Out of the Fire

A Calaveras Anthology

Manzanita Writers Press
Angels Camp, California
manzapress.com

Manzanita Writers Press

Out of the Fire
©2017

Suzanne Murphy – Editor
Monika Rose – Co-Editor
Joy Roberts – Finance Director
Joyce Dedini – Book Design and Layout

Cover Photo: *Dragon* by John Slot.
     Butte fire photo taken Wednesday, September 9, 2015 at 8:35 PM.
Title Page Art: *Beyond the Fire* by Cate Culver. Multimedia on wood.

Publisher: Manzanita Writers Press
1211 South Main Street
PO Box 460, Angels Camp, CA 95222
manzapress.com
manzanitawp@gmail.com

Other books by Manzanita Writers Press:

Entente–Irish Clans – Book 2 in the Series by Stephen Finlay Archer
Searchers–Irish Clans – Book 1 in the Series by Stephen Finlay Archer
Pieces Vignettes: Melding Memory Out of the Fire chapbook–Edited by Monika Rose
Too Much to Swallow by Glenn Wasson
Tales Mark Twain Would Have Loved to Steal by Glenn Wasson
Chance: A Jockey's Odyssey by Franklin Ted Laskin
George A. Custer, Please Come to the White Courtesy Phone by Franklin Ted Laskin
Copper Dawn by Dave Self
A Taste of Literary Elegance: Wine, Cheese & Chocolate–Edited by Monika Rose
Wild Edges–Edited by Monika Rose
Manzanita: Poetry and Prose of the Mother Lode & Sierra, Volumes 1-5

ISBN: 978-0-9968858-1-2
Printed in the United States of America

Editors' Notes

The *Out of the Fire* anthology, a collection of written and visual art primarily from the Calaveras County community, has been a natural outcome of the human need to share stories. At the height of the Butte Fire destruction and then into the following days and months of rescue and recovery, people gathered to comfort one another, restore hope, and share their experiences. Manzanita Writers Press put into motion a project to provide blog space for all community members to submit writing, photo art, and images that tell their stories, with the intention that a curated collection in a published anthology would appear in 2017 with a web site to follow. At the same time, artists Robin Modlin and Anne Cook, through a Calaveras County Arts Council grant, created a mosaic project called Pieces, readying burned and broken relics such as pottery bits, pieces of tools, household implements, and other objects to use as texture for the memorial wall in Mountain Ranch. The artists contacted Manzanita Writers Press (MWP) asking whether affiliated authors would write original stories based on their arrangements of artifacts salvaged from blasted homes and properties. The resulting poetry and prose were published by MWP in the "Pieces Vignettes" chapbook, accompanying photos by Will Mosgrove. The Out of the Fire blog, housed on the Manzanita Writers Press website, continues to accept submissions from community members in order to document an ongoing record of the impact of the fire on the Calaveras Community.

Suzanne Murphy

Narrowly escaping the Butte Fire that singed our family property, after enduring many other threats from fires over the last twenty-five years within a three-mile radius of our home, I was once again reminded of the fragility of our living space and the beauty of the region, achingly lost for many people whose houses and the natural landscape of their property and vistas burned. The healing mission of the Butte Fire anthology was born within a month of the destructive conflagration. We set to work the end of September 2015, planning healing writing sessions, art therapy, and creating a record of the event through the power of story and poetry and art. Out of destruction can come despair, but then the green shoot of hope works its way into the mix. That must be what happened with us. We felt an overwhelming desire to create an artistic home for artists, writers, musicians, historians, and the equally creative public appreciation for such a place spurred the editors of Manzanita Writers Press to house their artistic endeavors in Angels Camp. Manzanita Arts Emporium came into existence to create a safe, friendly, and beautiful haven for visitors to our region and locals and residents alike. Our mission is to provide a positive literary, artistic, educational, historical, and cultural environment for the community, and this anthology continues our long tradition as a respected and supportive regional publisher.

Monika Rose

Out of the Fire Sponsors

$200 and Above
Anonymous donor from our community
Central Audubon Society
Ironstone Vineyards
Nancy Giddens
Signal Service

$100 - $199
Angels Camp Museum
Donna Becker
Calaveras County Library, San Andreas
Constance Corcoran
Julia Costello
Jim Fletcher
Denella Kimura
Little Owl's Cyber Security
David Richter
John & Michele Rugo
Ann Roberts Seely
Sheri Smith
Union Democrat
Glenn Wasson

$50 -$99
Denise Ancar and family
Stephen and Kathy Archer
James Bailey – in memory of Jan Overstreet
Wayne Carlson
Katie Clark
Anne K. Cook & Will Mosgrove
Cathryne Darmer
Rebecca Fischer
Anne Forrest
Lou Gonzalez
Lara Grant
Karen Harper
Cheri Q. Holmes
Hotel Leger
Dave Houck
Robin Modlin
Renee Ramig
Cynthia Restivo
Joy C. Roberts
Jackie Rogers
Gary Rose

$50 -$99
Gail Stark
Charleen Tyson
Volunteer Center Calaveras County
Joy Willow
Allison Wright
Janice Zellers

$25 -$49
Backcountry Pictures
Sy Baldwin
Kathleen Ball
Teresa Borden
Kevin Brady & Marta Johnson
Cliff Bennett
Jen Bruneel
Claudette Cervinka
Myrna Doering
Brent Duffin
Trish Frazier
June Augusta Gillam
Susan M. Harrison
David Katz
Jennifer La
Darcy Lambert
Glenna Larson
Anthony J. Marinelli
Shanda McGrew
Bob Middleton
Pam Mundale
Maryan Newbury
Rosalie Nicholson
Ray Pezzi
Laura Pintane
Debbie Ponte
Nitya Prema
Sharon Reyes
Frank Santos
Selma Sattin & Robert Baird
Dave Self
Tim Smith
Ann Williams

"BUTTE FIRE"
AMADOR and CALAVERAS COUNTIES
SEPTEMBER 9TH - OCTOBER 1ST 2015
70,868 ACRES DESTROYED
549 HOMES DESTROYED
2 CIVILIAN DEATHS
LOSS of LIVESTOCK UNDETERMINED

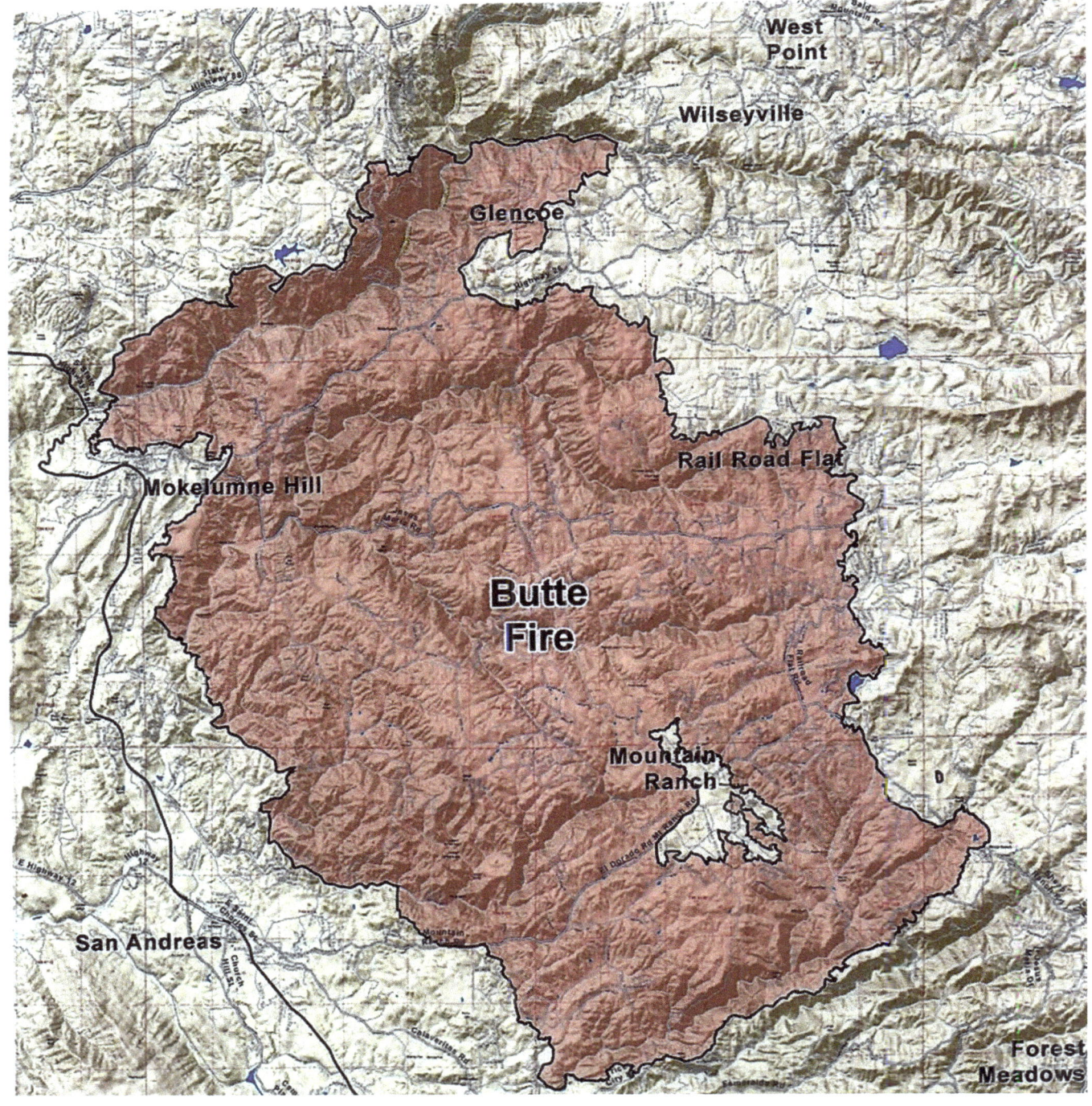

Incident Map Courtesy of CAL FIRE @ CAL.FIRE.com

Table of Contents

Ty Childress

Devil Fire Warrior
Wayne Carlson

The Warrior, a Tribute
Sydney Avey

He jumps the canyon rim,
fist pumps the air, bellows belligerent smoke
and descends like a marauder
to bully the dry forest
rooted and mute in his path.

We scamper from disturbed nests,
form columns, arm ourselves
with courage and technology.
He stomps through, keeps going.

His savage face paints
across miles of sky
Heart hot and black
pumped with stolen oxygen
driven by a century-old hunger,
he devours acres of brush,
picks his teeth with the tops of trees,
and pulls his dragon tail deftly
out of harm's way.

We bring in reinforcements,
buzz his head, use our diplomacy,
invite him to go elsewhere.
He will go wherever he pleases.

His specter rises in clouds
open-mawed, empty-eyed,
an ancient soul named Legion.
He will go, but not before he has
skinned our forest,
seared our lungs,
and settled the score.

Devil in the Sky
Wayne Carlson

Rising From The Ashes: New Life Begins Again

by Kathleen A. Ball

We arrived at sunset to see the blackened earth and charred trees which were the remains of years of happiness, abundant gardens of food, flowers, Japanese maples, oaks and pines, my studio, my husband's shop, and our home. But instead of seeing the destruction all around me, what I noticed as I looked out over the horizon, were the most glorious reds, oranges and magentas I had ever seen. I was mesmerized by the beauty of the sunset view in the midst of the ashes. As my gaze fell to the earth below, where my entryway once stood, the bronze heads of Leonardo da Vinci and Willie Nelson, held high above the shard remains, were a sharp contrast to the bits and pieces of china, mangled wires, and smoke. Oddly, I was filled with a feeling of freedom, when looking upon the ashes of almost sixty years of life. Remains of thousands of books, that consumed as many of hours of study, in search of truth, a Master's and finally a Doctorate, gone — the foundations of my life's work as an artist and professor of art. Thousands of hours of lecture notes, course curricula and boxes and boxes of demos and teaching supplies — poof, all gone in a puff of smoke. I stood there contemplating what to do with this clear slate. Teaching again would be highly unlikely without my notes, supplies, and slides. It would take years to replace those things. Besides, I'd already reaped the benefits and joy from the years I taught, in every moment of creation, finding great books and supplies for my students and the exhilaration I felt when they created a work of art for the first time. It was an honor few people ever experience. I knew in my heart that I would now take all my life experiences and create a very different future.

Two years before the fire, I had my first "clear slate" experience. I went on a journey into the Amazon jungle in Peru to participate in a ten-day ancient healing, ceremonial retreat to heal myself of cancerous tumors in my liver. To prepare for this healing, it was necessary to completely rid myself of all attachments. To accomplish this, I meditated for several weeks prior to the trip, visualizing who I would be if I weren't a wife, mother, teacher, artist, TV show host or all the other titles I'd adopted through the years. The woman who entered the ceremonies was just a soul searching for wholeness. When I returned to the States for a CT scan, the test revealed that I was cancer-free.

After only nine months, I had again developed tumors in my liver. Another surrender, this time in Brazil in August 2015. I traveled to many beautiful cities and met with shamans and healers, and participated in meditations with Hindu masters, yogi and Sufi masters who assisted me on my spiritual journey. Little did I know that this journey would set the foundation for the rest of my life, preparing me for what was soon to come.

Maggie Sloan

Ponderosa Way
John Slot

I returned from Brazil, having come to peace with everything. I sat in meditation and contemplated a sculpting job I'd been offered in Alta Paraiso, as well as the possibility of a liver transplant. For nine days I considered my options. I felt encumbered by the thought of having to sort through everything if my husband and I chose to move to Brazil.

While I was still thinking of my future options, the smoke from the Butte fire thickened in the skies above us, working its way through Mokeulumne Hill to Pine Grove and Glencoe. We sat tight, listening to the firefighter reports advising us not to worry about evacuation. By Thursday, September 10th, I felt increasingly uneasy all through the day as the authorities continued to advise us not to worry. We'd rounded up our kitties, Pi, Chatom Jolie, Meritaten and Tiya and had them all in the house, their carriers handy, important papers, the silver, and a few mementos, just in case. But we didn't think we were leaving until we heard the knock on the door. Our nephew Cody had arrived with a few friends, beckoning us outside. We saw 250-foot flames coming over the ridge behind our garage, and it shook us to the marrow. Pretty impressive and quite motivating.

Carnage
Kent Lambert

11

Throwing what we could in the cars, we frantically scrambled out the door of our house. As we sped toward our cabin in Garden City, I was certain that we would never see our house again. And I was right. Thank goodness we had a place to stay, unlike so many others who were left completely stranded in tents and cars in the Mountain Ranch Park. I felt extremely lucky.

After that night, everything happened so quickly that I barely recall the details. They involved insurance companies and fire agencies, FEMA and Red Cross, and, of course, my liver doctors. In the midst of it, we had to relocate into something winter-worthy, which meant moving again. Fortunately, one of our amazing and very dear friends, Marci Biagi, lent us a rental unit in the nick of time. Then in the middle of dealing with the mundane tasks of replacing clothing, toothbrushes, and birth certificates, my doctor called me in for

Kent Lambert

an additional CT scan. Lo and behold, another two new rapid-growing tumors. I looked the doctor square in the eye and said, "Take it, I'm ready." So the morning of November 5th, I awoke with a brand-new liver, surrounded by doctors, my husband, my loving family and dear friends.

My birthday gift the next year was moving into our new home in Pine Grove. The joyful and fun-filled process of decorating it began. Built around the skeletons of the few possessions we had managed to stuff in our vehicles when we'd left with the fire on our heels, we created our new home.

Before the fire I had been a prolific sculptor for over forty years, but I had very few of my works of art left and no clay, no kilns, and no tools. Off to the art supply I went, but I came away with painting supplies instead. Then began a flood of new creations. I made over fifteen paintings in three months after the fire. The first one I titled, "Rising From the Ashes."

After settling in and giving my body time to recover, I have returned to those earlier contemplations of what I should do with my remaining years. What gives my soul joy? My answer to the questions regarding my future that had been arising from my soul, beginning only days before the fire, and in the months afterward, presented itself with absolutely no struggle or labor whatsoever. It had appeared before me as a magic carpet arrives on the breeze from the heavens. Resuming my travels, or returning to Brazil, would be so thrilling, but missing my family would be an issue. My grandchildren are my pride and joy, and now I wanted to spend my time with them.

With the circle now complete, the rebirth in progress, I am filled with humility and reverence. Life is an ongoing process so exquisitely full of excitement and renewal, I can't imagine missing a single moment.

Rising from the Ashes
Kathleen Ball

Wayne Carlson

Maria Camillo

California Fires 2015
Donna Becker

Sun through smoke
makes a pallid orange shadow,
Sunrises and sunsets, which might be glorious,
are a sinister pink.
Each leaf, usually a gift of green and grace,
is now only desiccated brown fuel.
The thin smell of smoke
stops me,
makes me alert like an animal,
smoke carried for miles,
or maybe nearer.
The sound of each plane and helicopter
a possible harbinger,
Tiny fragments of black ash
on the wind —
someone's home burned and scattered,
flying in pieces high in the atmosphere
landing here.
The breeze warm on my skin
shakes the dry leaves in warning.

Fly Boys
John Slot

Debora Olguin

Our Mothers' Lamps Burned Up in the Butte Fire

Donna Becker

I like to think of the lamp
that stood so many years
at my mother's bedside,
the red flower painted
Sears reproduction
of a kerosene lamp
from an earlier age.
I think it reminded my mother
of the nights in
her aunt's cold farmhouse.
The lamp found no place in my home
but happily, it did in yours.
That lamp in your cabin,
in your new quieter life.
"Just right,"
you said.

Your two lamps were
of fine pale green porcelain
painted and gilded
with more delicate flowers,
silken shades.
One sent to the restorer
at great cost
after the cousin's dog
knocked it into pieces.

These lamps of our mothers' evenings,
which they loved for the
glowing prettiness.
Their hands each night
turned the knobs
to darkness
in a way
we love to remember.

Fire Angel
Anne Cook

Sifting Ashes

For Richard and Gail

Helen Bonner

John Slot

After the fire, the Butte Fire, the brute fire,
raged through our woods—
         wild, hell-raising beast, devouring all—
We waited while it cooled,
And waited
         till our hearts could bear to see
         there was nothing to see
         of all that had once been
         Everything.
Woods, house, cars, gardens, paintings, tools,
All the beauty we had built together.
         Gone.

Then we waded in to sift the ashes, found
a coin collection, jewelry, cufflinks—badges of success,
buried in the charred pile
that once had been
a mahogany desk.

Beyond the metal skeleton of a flower-arched gate
where our garden had flourished,
a sculpted lion, proud as ever,
a brassy praying angel,
a serene Buddha
survey the blackened earth.
If you asked them, they would say,
Look at each other.
You have everything.

Michelle Bellinger

19

Asparagus
Kent Lambert

Looking Back
Then and Now . . .

Jesus Maria Road

Summer 2010
Wayne Carlson

Jesus Maria Road

August 2016
Wayne Carlson

One Butte Fire Story
by Wayne Carlson

Wednesday, September 9, 2015   11:00 pm.

It was the fourth story on the 11:00 news. "A 150-acre fire is now being responded to in Amador County just east of Butte Mountain." Wow, kind of close, I thought. I'm sure it'll be out by morning. The news channel failed to mention that the actual acreage being consumed at this point was approximately 14,500 acres.

Thursday, September 10, 2015   9:00 am.

My coffee in hand, I turn on the local morning news. Now the fire is the second story. "The Amador County fire has grown to 6000 acres (again, the newsroom was unaware of the actual acreage, somewhere between 14,500 and 20,000 acres at this point) and appears to be burning out of control. Burning southwest towards Calaveras County." I thought that 6000 acres was pretty big for just overnight. It's coming our way, but again, I am confident and complacent that Cal Fire and other resources will take care of it. By 2 pm, it is apparent that there will be a major problem. The sky began to change drastically over our area, Railroad Flat. It moved toward us with what seemed like amazing speed. At the end of this day, it is raging, consuming approximately 32,000 acres, growing and out of control. We are evacuated at 5 pm today. My wife Kim and I stayed with friends in Ione, California, thirty-three miles from our home, for the next ten days. The adrenaline in me was constant.

Wayne Carlson

Friday, September 11, 2015

The fire exploded to over 64,000 acres, and in the next twenty-one days, life as we knew it here in the foothills would change forever in many ways. An incredible event, surrealistic at the least, unbelievable in its devastation, In total, 70,868 acres were destroyed. In the end, fully contained by October 1, 2015, it was to become the seventh-largest fire in California history.

September 13, 2015   Day Four

The combined efforts by all of the incident partners involved, morning, noon, and night was a scene, for me, of high-level adrenaline. After my morning attendance at the daily "fire briefings" inside the Jackson Rancheria Hotel, I would drive all around the fire areas in my truck. The intersection at Highway 88 and Highway 26, located in Mokelumne Hill, was a staging area for PG&E workers, who stacked a hundred or so new power poles about every other day, in readiness for replacement of the destroyed ones. Cal Fire, refueled service fuel vehicles and trucks here at Sierra Market. Local volunteers got around in off-road vehicles, and the media were doing interviews.

I drove eight miles south on Highway 88 to San Andreas, which at times was considered to be in imminent danger during the daily firefights. Rumors swirled all around that San Andreas had caught fire. It did not. Mountain Ranch Road in San Andreas was shut shut down at Mark Twain Hospital. Nobody could go any farther toward Mountain Ranch, another eight miles up the road. Jesus Maria Road, from Highway 26 in Mokelumne Hill to Railroad Flat Road in Mountain Ranch, a distance of nine miles, was completely closed the second day. This stretch of nine miles was to become the south center of the fire.

On the ground, PG&E trucks, Cal Fire trucks, water tenders were in constant movement everywhere. Chinook helicopters carried 2600-gallon water buckets dangling underneath them to affected areas, and air tankers delivered fire retardant across more than 60,000 acres. Incredible efforts.

In the initial days, what seemed like hundreds of livestock trailers, one after the other, ran back and forth along Highway 88 around Jackson. People were racing against time to save their livestock, their animals. There wasn't enough time to save them all. This was a devastating loss of wildlife, livestock, and landscape. I chatted with a local rancher, a distraught woman who was forced to simply free her horses onto her property, in the faint hope they might find their way to safety. She was crying to me as she related her inability to secure safety for all her animals. These animals, this livestock, for many people, this is their family. Their losses were uncountable in the end.

I was helpless in the middle of the ongoing death and destruction of all this wildlife, livestock, and landscape. My thoughts were always that this must end quickly. Then I looked southeast over the top of Sierra Market, there at the intersection of Highways 26 and 88 in the near distance, and I saw the flames rage on. There would be seventeen days of fighting before the Butte Fire would be officially 100% contained on October 1, 2015.

Saturday, September 19, 2015

People are now living in trailers and tents, scattered everywhere along Mountain Ranch Road, Railroad Flat Road, and the town of Mountain Ranch. Returnees to what was once their homes, their security, their lives, are seen wandering around with a stony gaze at the ashes of their lives. Looking everywhere. Staring at the ground aimlessly for something, trying to take in this heartbreaking loss while trying to connect with a personal item, as if to validate it is their life's ashes they are actually standing in. A broken piece of china, a burned metal picture frame, a partially charred child's toy. A material part of their life destroyed by this disaster. Yet wanting to connect with something. A memory, to touch it, to pick it up. Everything else is gone.

Wayne Carlson

Ty Childress

A Perspective on the Butte Fire
Katie Clark

The following are excerpts from her blog posts about the first days of the Butte Fire.

Greg and I were on vacation in Tahoe and planned to meet my mom in Reno on Wednesday night, September 9. While we were out with her, I got an alert on my phone from the local news on KCRA3, noting a fire near Mokelumne Hill. I sent my dad a quick email, "See smoke yet?" Then everything spiraled into a nightmare.

When I called my dad again later to talk, he was already thinking of things to locate and pack if needed. We had moved to Mountain Ranch in 1990 and had packed in preparation for evacuations three times before, but we never had to leave. Though I no longer lived in this house, it had been the only family home I knew. I told my dad that in the worst case, we were insured to the hilt and it would be okay. He didn't seem to appreciate that comment. It wasn't as comforting as I thought.

I kept an eye on the news and Facebook groups I belong to, and I stayed on top of the fire all night.

By the second day, the fire had exploded overnight. We couldn't sit there and do nothing. That afternoon, I started a fundraiser campaign on the gofundme site to raise money for supplies to evacuees. I knew that the evacuation was going to continue and not resolve quickly. While we continued with our Thursday plans to spend the day in Virginia City, Nevada, I was glued all that time to my phone. At this point, there were posts on Facebook everywhere similar to the following:

I am being evacuated, I have 6 horses,
a 500lb pig and two dogs.
I only have one horse trailer.
Please help 209-xxx-xxxx.

I had to let my donkeys and horse go,
I could not get them out in time.
If you see them, please call me. Photo below.

Then I began to see:
I have a five horse trailer and
am driving in from Clements now,
call me if you need help 209 xxx-xxxx.

I have 10 acres, all fenced for livestock.
We have an extra guest quarters and
room for a couple dogs.
Please call us if you need space,
in Valley Springs!

Attention! There are 50 horse trailers
currently staging at Raleys, if anyone
needs evacuation, CALL US NOW!
Don't wait until it's too late 209-xxx-xxxx.

I commented, posted, and followed everything I could. I was seeing all the calls for help pouring out from my hometown community. I watched as friend after friend posted that they had to leave their homes. Donations were already starting to come in through gofundme.

My mom got back home that day. She and my dad immediately began packing. He told us he wouldn't believe any of the news—and then he saw a singed leaf fall from the sky. Next would come hot embers. A neighbor later told me that as her husband calmly told her to stock the fridge in their RV, he saw flames cresting the hill.

My parents left before the mandatory evacuations were put out in their area. My mom could hear propane tanks exploding over the ridge as they left. They took two of the vehicles, all the possessions they could, and our Dalmatian, Gabriella. That night they stayed at my mom's insurance agency office. I felt helpless.

On the third day, I had been watching on-line news of the evacuation centers and paid attention to the items that were needed. I started making a shopping list. My lifelong friend, whose own twin sister had been evacuated, went with me to Costco and helped us spend $1,200 at Costco and fill three carts. My mom had also called ahead, and the manager donated $100 towards our purchase.

We were able to provide pajamas and toiletries to an entire group home of twenty teenage boys who had been evacuated and had nothing. As they helped us unload the car, one boy said it was "like Christmas," and they were overjoyed to just have some deodorant and new clothes. We went next door to the Veteran's Hall in Valley Springs. They were just setting up to be an evacuation center and shortly expected as many as one hundred evacuated seniors from San Andreas. They had very few supplies, so left with them the items and food products we could and put out the word on Facebook that they needed more.

We then continued out to the campsites set up at New Hogan Reservoir. We located a drop-off donation center, which was no more than two women at two picnic tables with items. We gave them a good portion of our supplies. The women had been out there all day and needed to go home to their children. I promised I'd put the word out on Facebook that they needed relief. While we were there, I met two people from my hometown of Mountain Ranch. I spoke with both of them, and offered them hugs and strength. We then had to continue on.

We couldn't drive through San Andreas on the fourth day, so we took the long way from Valley Springs down to Copperopolis and up to Frog Town in Angels Camp. The county fairgrounds there had been converted into a huge evacuation center and fire staging area with room for a large number of animals. There were animals everywhere, volunteers doing all they could, and vets running around caring for all these pets and livestock. We unloaded the remainder of the supplies we had at the fairgrounds.

That evening we learned that nobody had heard from my dad's best friend. He lived near us, and when he last spoke with my dad, he said he wasn't coming down off the hill. His family and daughters were worried, and my parents were worried. I tracked down a photograph of him, got his vitals from my mom, and went to work posting a plea for help in locating him. We were confident he was safe but just unsure of where he was. People were to be on the lookout for a man with a nifty handlebar mustache, a red jeep, and a Shepherd- looking dog named Pisser. The post was shared hundreds of times, and within hours I had someone whose boyfriend recognized the photograph. The boyfriend had been back in the evacuated area on a quad in the afternoon and remembered seeing a man with a jeep and a dog. The next day, my dad's missing friend found a phone to call his daughter and let her know he was okay. It turned out, the boyfriend had gone back to tell the man that his family and fiends were worried, so he needed to call them.

The fire still continues, and there's a lot left to do.

Calaveras is not a land of
weak individuals or quitters.
This will not keep us down.
We will not quit until everyone
is back where they need to be.
This effort will continue.

Highway 26 Revisited
Constance J. Corcoran

Eight black and white miles of skeleton-treed road wind up the ridge south of the river. Charcoal landscape starts at Happy Valley. The ruins of Boston Yale Ranch are exposed. An old cowhand's cabin survives where the water ditch used to cross. Places I knew as Lawson's and Robinson's are surrounded by stark black ground. Past the cow pond and charred pasture, I pull into a burnt dirt driveway.

Wet ash makes my eyes run. Grandma's house is marked by a melted refrigerator, tangled bedsprings, and the foundation. Up the hill, strands of wire dangle from charcoal posts that once framed my uncle's dog kennels. Through a tangle of leafy branches, I see my childhood home. It is layered with different versions of siding now, and raised up on a real foundation, but the windows are in the same places as the pictures and my memories. Two old stumps were linden trees that suspended my rope swing. Fresher cuts made days ago saved the house.

Grandma's Cabin
Courtesy of Constance J. Corcoran

The homeowner stands in her open doorway, phone in hand.

My family built these houses in 1948, I explain. *I had to see it.*

Sure, take a look. She graciously walks with me. *We could never find out which house was built first.* She is eager to hear.

* * * *

We told the story over and over my whole life. Our family came to California after the war for warmer weather and jobs. Before I was a year old, Mom's brothers and mother migrated from Galesburg, Illinois, where they all were born and raised. While working at Mare Island, Dad met a man who said there were jobs in the sawmill at Wilseyville, in the heart of the Sierra Nevada. So we followed the Mokelumne River through the Delta into Calaveras County's foothills.

Local rancher Carl Dell'Orto sold to Dad and Mom's brother Dick four acres from a corner of his winter pastureland east of Mokelumne Hill in an area known as Rich Gulch. It had been a prosperous mining camp in the late 1850s. Over time, they paid $200 for the property from their Associated Lumber and Box wages.

Dad and the uncles brought scrap lumber from the mill. They salvaged iron from an abandoned gold mine near our property to make plumbing. They witched for water and then blasted a well, using old dynamite they'd found under a miner's cabin.

Greenhorns! I don't know how we survived, said my uncle.

While the grownups built, my brother Johnny and I collected rusty square-headed nails that sifted up from the red dust, evidence that our homestead once had been a stagecoach stop.

My House 1949
Courtesy of Constance J. Corcoran

Our house was nearest the highway, now named the *Stephen P. Teale Memorial Highway* in honor of our family doctor, Doc Teale, who later became a State Senator. He would stop by the house to check up on my mother when she was pregnant with my baby brother. I watched the ash grow on the end of his cigar as he bent over Mom's belly.

My older brother and I shared bunk beds on the back porch, where Mom read to us every night and Johnny sang songs he made up while trying to fall asleep. Dad later added a deck that extended along the gully side of the house. After my brother Chris was born, the deck was closed in with a wall of windows. It served first as a dining room and finally my room. Mom and Dad's room was off the ever-changing combination living-dining-kitchen area. Walls went up and walls came down to make larger or smaller rooms.

Carl got Dick a ditch-tender job at Camp Four off Lower Dorray Road, just up the Highway. The pay included a cabin, living quarters for Dick and Grandma until their house was built. Grandma hauled water from the ditch for bathing and cooking. She washed her clothes in a bucket, hanging wet laundry to dry on a manzanita bush.

We had to pack in, said Uncle Dick, *supplies, food, everything. There was only a narrow dirt path from the road to the cabin.*

Uncle Dick built his and Grandma's house across the lower end of the gulch, a drainage that cut our four acres in two. He added a footbridge across Wet Gulch, so named for the muddy slough it became during rainy season. In summer, Wet Gulch baked to hard clay, and we made tunnels in the chest-high wheat grass.

A tall stand of Scotch thistles grew along our approach to the footbridge, near the outhouse. Some people deliberately add these plants to rock gardens for the large purple flower, but those thorny leaves had a real bite. My strongest memory of them is the outhouse smell.

Uncle George built a square white house with a wraparound porch directly across the upper gully from us. We sent messages back and forth to our cousins on a pulley clothesline that extended from our back stoop across to their porch. That house was replaced some time ago by a newer one, built by a stranger. It

Grandma's House 1952
Courtesy of Constance J. Corcoran

29

too has survived the fire.

I thought Grandma's house was the nicest on the homestead. Painted light yellow, it had a pitched roof and front and back porches. Grandma would sit in her rocker with a crocheted afghan across her shoulders, while visitors shared a small sofa or claimed the overstuffed chair. Her own grandmother's mahogany spinet desk and a music box were treasured family heirlooms. A Seth Thomas mantle clock softly gonged the hour as we studied *Scrabble* letters or worked a jigsaw puzzle. An oval braid rug warmed her knotty pine floor.

While washing supper dishes, Grandma stood at her kitchen window to watch the sun set over the pond, listening to classical music, smoking her Raleigh cigarettes that she *did not inhale*. Afterward, Grandma and I walked across Carl's pasture to the pond and back, taking her daily *constitutional*, with the cat and her Airedale Koty. She liked to pretend she hated the cat, but we couldn't go without him. Sometimes we walked farther, following the dirt road to a hunter's cabin.

Twice a year I ran to the highway to watch cowboys driving Carl's herd from winter pastures to the high country in spring and down again in the fall. When the herd was pastured next to us, the clanking of cowbells soothed me to sleep.

Fields away on our southwest horizon, two cypress trees marked the gates of an old pioneer cemetery on a property we knew as Lockheed's. The buildings had burned long before and the people left. We enjoyed picking from their apple trees in the fall.

Mom used to drive my brothers and me down the lower Ponderosa Road, near Robinson's. She took our old Chevy while Dad was at work. No four-wheel drive needed. In August we picked blackberries at a wide bend in the road. I learned to swim under the bridge on the Mokelumne River, just above the dam on Electra Road, close to where the fire started.

When Uncle Dick married, he sold the yellow house. The family came together for one last construction project when we built Grandma a small cabin on our side of the gully, just

Grandma's House 2015
Courtesy of Constance J. Corcoran

behind our house. My job was to sit on the sawhorse and hold boards steady while Dad cut or to walk under the raised floor to pick up nails for reuse. I even got to pound nails in some of the floorboards until everyone saw how many dents I made.

Mom said that house was the last straw — the worst of all the houses we built. It was my favorite project because I was old enough to participate. Now a truck carcass, bulldozed during the firefight, covers its sooty remains.

By 1959 sawmills in the foothills were struggling. Dad's job at Associated came to an end. We left the family compound for the suburbs of Sacramento, where there was work in the aerospace industry.

It is a lifetime since I left Rich Gulch. Before the fire, our homestead had become littered with rusty vehicles, broken appliances, and cast-offs from a succession of occupants. An oleander thicket along the highway hid the houses.

Lower Dorray Road today is red with fire retardant. This is the first time I've been able to see the river from here. Now a seared landscape reveals too much. The property is too clean. Views across the county are too vast. Cypress trees no longer mark an old pioneer cemetery. My house has lost its family.

Gordon Long

Maria Camillo

Ty Childress

Ty Childress

Art and the World
Cate Culver

I am an artist, a painter whose art burned up in the homes of my Mountain Ranch community. I create art to lift the world. I didn't always know this. People who bought my art and took it to their homes told me this.

One owner of my art says, "Every morning as I sit and put on my shoes, I rest my eyes on the flowing stream you painted. The art is above my bed. The water flowing over rocks, grounds me before I start my day." Another owner tells me, "Your painting of the red beets and flowing green leaves is in my kitchen. The colors are so vibrant, when I am tired somehow your art keeps me going."

To lift the world is not like painting angels or sunrises. It is more like creating a piece of art that smiles back. It is one of life's simple pleasures that feeds you daily. It gives the viewer a lift in spirit.

When art is destroyed, the smile is gone. Its positive energy has been transformed. Where did it go? Up in smoke that spreads across the earth and is gone. It saddens me that this original creation is no more, and I cannot make another that is the same.

However, my loss is small. Others lost their past.

Rough Ride
Anne Cook

Retirement

Pam Dunn

Sarah and her husband were looking at retirement property on California's central coast when they heard the Butte fire had jumped from Amador to Calaveras County. When they left Thursday morning, they thought the fire was out, but by Thursday evening the town of Mokelumne Hill had been evacuated. By Friday, they began making phone calls, and Sarah's friends told her that their neighborhood was in flames.

After years of working in stressful jobs, they were living the back-to-the-land existence they'd always talked about. At first, she had the energy of a Gold Rush settler. She and her husband whacked and burned, recovered from poison oak rashes, dealt with star thistle, chaparral, and an overgrown ten acres that needed reclaiming. When it snowed in those days, it seemed a mere skiff, a dusting on the ground that vanished the next day. They'd remained full of rural romanticism. Washing lettuce leaves one at a time. Swiping earwigs and sow bugs down the drain.

In later years, she'd proven not to be up to the toil. Everything began to weigh on her. Their particular elevation seemed to be nice only in two seasons, spring and fall. Lately, you could snap your fingers and miss the mountain's golden poppies and the fall's autumn colors. During the summer fires, she drove though billowing smoke and hot ash, flames on both sides of the highway. In the winter, inching along "S" bends around wrecked and stranded vehicles, she feared that sudden slip that would match the skip in her heart. The loading of wood into the stove, vacuuming spider webs, canning garden vegetables, and listening to O.E.S. bulletins about the latest wildfire or winter storm—it hit her in a horrible sort of way that there was no point to any of it.

The last time the power went out, her husband carried the flashlight, revealing an aged, craggy face she didn't recognize. The flashlight's beam played around the room, bringing out the shapes of things. Then he went out to start the generator that ran the pump and refrigerator. She realized if he died, she would be cut off, helpless. It must have been at that moment, when she began to doubt their retirement plans.

In September, it was over one hundred degrees on California's central coast.

They'd looked at several retirement communities there in one day. Back in the hotel, she Googled the latest Butte fire results. Fire

Ty Childress

had a different language. Containment in percentages. Fire lines. Nights you prayed for cool downs so the firefighters could get an edge. This time, the fire was raging in the Jesus Maria Canyon—moving so fast and hot, the flames were chasing people from their homes.

On television they watched firestorms that looked like tornados. Homes they recognized were burning, trees were exploding like bombs. When they arrived in Calaveras County on Saturday, gray smoke and hot ash billowed across the road, the sky streaked red and black. Fire trucks parked everywhere along the main highway. Helicopters carrying water buckets churned overhead. The road to their home was blocked.

"Did you have animals?" a worker at Red Cross asked them.

"No, just stray cats," Sarah answered. Both of the cats they had brought with them from civilization were long gone now. One got old and died, and the neighbors' dogs killed the other one.

The next day they told their insurance company they had no idea if they would be coming back to anything. Then Sarah and her husband went shopping for a cell phone and clothes. Everything they owned was in their suitcase. Oddly enough, they had their swimming suits.

The few friends they contacted reported the same thing: their homes were gone. They began to fear the worst. They ate at cafes and watched the television hoping for some change that would slow the fire's path. Of course, their particular area had weather cycles that were impossible to predict. There had been five years of hot weather and drought when the foothills went up like flaming fireballs. Usually the rainy seasons brought torrential rains, impassible roads, and floods in the lowlands.

This last season had no spring and a foot of snow in April. At the motel, she thought about pulling the covers over her head until the fire burned itself out, when she might venture forth again without this painful fear lodging in her chest.

It was a week before they were finally allowed onto the property.

Along Mountain Ranch Road, the land was burned, homes were gone, but the town itself had survived. Their hope began to build. And then three miles beyond, they entered the canyon areas. The blackened trees were still standing. Homes had turned to ash. At the end of the gravel drive, their truck, sitting

Ladybug Screw
Kent Lambert

35

Wheelbarrow
Kent Lambert

on metal rims, looked like a heap of junk, the tires vaporized. The storage sheds and pump house were nothing but rubble. Sarah was too stunned to speak. The accumulations of a lifetime were gone. She could make out parts of things: the couch's springs and a hulk that might have been the kitchen range. Everything thing else had been turned to ash or was buried underneath the ashes. Charred and blackened, the wood stove had been hurled to the ground.

They looked at the outline of their house.

"It's burned down to the J-bolts sticking out of the foundation," her husband said.

She stood looking at all of her world. She tasted dust and smelled the burn. And yet, she recalled why they had bought the place, what it had meant to her. She began to cry and her husband came to her and hugged her close.

They would start over.

Ty Childress

Gordon Long

Smoke and Mirrors
Kat Everitt

trapped in this house upcountry for days
car packed with only the essentials
only these raggedy memories that will fit
lord knows we cried so carefully
for we were not on fire
not even evacuated though many
of our old neighbors in The Meadows
had gone down from the mountain
at the first sign of smoke and there it is:
smoke. smoke. smoke. for days
pale yellow skies in smoke. silence.
the silence is silver in the smoke and
mirrors all around us like the zombie
invasion set of some ole B movie
from an imagined childhood where all
is supposed to be well
and houses do not ever burn down
oh, will you look at that? the fire is only
four miles away and our neighbor can see
its glow from the ridge. so, course,
they are going to go on down to the valley
where all of this is just a story told to be
sad and to write "Heart with you, Friend"
on totally crowded social media because,
like bees, we are gathering what honey
we can, checking every hour or so with
the sheriff's department, Should we leave?
Is the Evacuation Advisement in place?
just like bees leaving the hive in chaos,
fearful of the smoke-oils on the mirrors
all around us, reflecting our slim courage
leaving in our dreams. leaving for real

because we can, because, we still can

Gordon Long

Stronger Than Fire
Kat Everitt

After the fire
passes through mountains
colors of autumn
songs of the jays in the still and dry air
black hills with less life
waiting for waters
a bursting of seeds where
these fires rampaged
and you are a witness
to all that is golden
as much as a witness
to all that is dear
and you speak of truths
about trees with no life now
and truths about trees
that are still living here
we take and we give
the earth gives more than we do
we are beggars just begging
for waters and souls
these stark autumn trees
beg in dignity's silence
for water's redemption
to sing our lives whole

Deborah Olguin

Facing the Monster
Rebecca Fischer

The billow of smoke towered over the horizon. Even miles away at Camanche, the plume was impressive, swirling, and ominous. Destructive.

"It looks like a monster," I told my uncle, who was sitting beside me in his old white Ford.

"It is a monster," was his simple reply.

A few days prior to this conversation, my uncle and I, with the help of one of our cowhands, had been working our cattle down by Camanche. We had stopped at El Torero in Burson for lunch. Sitting there looking out the window, I thought about the fire, the smoke. Despite our work, the fire was the main topic of conversation.

Then the call came from my dad. He had gotten word that the fire had spread to Jesus Maria, and could get to Hawver Road. He had cattle out there. We better go get them, as a precautionary measure.

Since my dad was on his way, we quickly finished our lunch. My uncle called a couple of his friends, leaving a voice message, "Looks like we're headed out there."

Would they hear it in time?

Hawver Road got its name from my grandmother's family; they had a ranch out there. It was never my favorite road. The break at the top of the hill—where it drops down into that narrow, steep, jagged section of road, rock to the left and air to the right—terrified me when I was a child. It was more terrifying that day, not because of the fire, but because of the traffic. Evacuees were racing out of there, since Hawver Road is one of the few safe exits from Jesus Maria. Meeting all those cars head-on with a gooseneck, a livestock trailer pulled by a truck, hampered our trek down. We were in their way, and they were in ours. Congested.

John Slot

A poorly-cut log partially blocked our way at a turn in the road. We took the turn extra wide and managed to inch past it.

Finally I made it down to the corral, the smoke billowing above me on the ridge. I was entranced by it as I swung up into my saddle. For a moment, I felt my insignificance in comparison. That thing could swallow me whole and spit me out, horse and all, charred and ruined. Yet the other cowhand and I chatted amiably about the fire as we stared into the eyes of the smoke. He believed the smoke was misleading, that the fire was farther away than it looked. I prayed the cattle weren't going to be difficult to get in the trailer. They like to run away from the corral, so I never look forward to working with them.

That day, though, my dad's cattle were cooperative. They were gathered together on one side of the hilly field, and they trotted right along the fence. One of our friends arrived and went on foot out into the field to turn the cattle into the pen, and for once they obliged. We had them in the corral within minutes of arriving, something that had never happened before.

There were about fifty head of cattle, plus the horses. That meant two trips with only three trailers. My uncle hadn't heard from his friends, and we weren't sure if they were coming. Hauling the cattle out was a good half-hour drive one way, especially with the traffic. A plane roared over us, so close I felt I could reach out and touch it. I looked at the remaining cattle in the pen. I wondered if we would have time to come back.

We loaded what we could and headed out. Unfortunately, the best place to turn around to drive back to San Andreas was up the road, toward Jesus Maria. My uncle and dad went up, but our friend, who was hauling the horses in his smaller trailer, figured out a way to turn around inside the corral.

As we drove up that narrow part in the road I don't like, we almost collided with two other friends, both pulling trailers. They had gotten my uncle's message. We took advantage of what little space the side of the road offered and pulled off to let them by. I jumped out and ran to the first truck to help them load and tell them how to turn around in the corral. And with that, I descended into the burning pit.

As we reached that tight turn with the log, an old van came blazing up, and barely avoided a collision with us. Now the van was in the space we needed to take the turn wide and miss the log. Inching by didn't work this time. The log caught the fender of the trailer and bent it. We could hear the tire rub it as we continued down Hawver Road. Miraculously, the tire didn't pop.

We met another vehicle shortly thereafter, a smaller red car that refused to back up and scooch to the side. Our friend managed to maneuver around the car, his agitation growing from his annoyance with the stubborn driver.

At last, we made it back to the hot corral. The two trailers were just big enough to load the remaining cattle. One trailer got caught on something again, this time on the corral, and broke one of the boards.

On our way out, I rode with our other friend, since he was the last out of the corral, and I had to close the gate for him. He lifted a small cooler bag from the back seat and offered me a cold drink. I hadn't noticed how parched I was until I guzzled it. The truck's temperature gauge read 107 degrees. I was sweating, and became aware of how badly I stank with

Wayne Carlson

body odor and smoke. Embarrassment rose in me, and I scolded myself, *Now is not the time to be self-conscious, Becca.*

As we drove up Hawver Road away from the corral, my eyes settled on a ragged old house, tucked up on the hillside. Tin roof, aged wood, chipping red paint. My great-grandparents had lived there; my grandmother and her sister grew up there. I felt my heart twist. A piece of my history. That house had survived so many long years. Would it survive the night? Another plane swooped over the ridge, this time depositing the bright red retardant right over the pine treetops. The fire had been closer than I thought. We opened a wire gate by the cattle guard, so that animals that had been turned loose could escape, if needed.

Back at the top of the hill, some evacuees had congregated to watch the hills burn, parking on both sides of the narrow road. It was difficult to squeeze between them with a trailer full of cattle. It was hard to understand why they didn't move so we could get out of there safely.

My uncle slept in his truck that night, out where we took the cattle. Even though we were quite a distance away, he got worried that the fire would jump Highway 49 and spread toward us again. We no longer questioned the spread of the fire. Even miles away, the flames lit up the night sky with an orange glow.

A few days later, when the fire was finally out and the roads opened, my family went out to the property to assess the damage. Aside from a couple of fences and some boards on the corral, the fire had moved around the barn and the house. Everything stood intact even though the fire had surrounded the place. We wondered how it had escaped destruction. While the retardant did help, we agreed the property survived because the cattle had eaten the grass down. No ember had floated in to alight on the aged wood to set it ablaze. Not one, and it could have done that so easily.

A cousin stopped by our main house to tell us with tears in his eyes that he had lost his home. There are many stories like his. To this day, some people are still in tents. Others are selling their scorched property. Some have rebuilt. And then there's this house. Tired, but unscathed.

It feels greedy to be thankful.

Michelle Bellinger

Butte Fire Blues
George Haskell

Woke up this morning
Made me want to cry
Forest home is burning
There's smoke up in the sky
I got the Butte Fire Blues
I got the Butte Fire Blues
Ain't nothin' been the same since the fire came rolling through

Smoke is rolling by me,
The flames are coming to
Gonna pack my load, get down the road
Before the burn comes roaring through
I got the Butte Fire Blues
I got the Butte Fire Blues
Ain't nothin' been the same since the fire came rolling through

Used to live in my big house
Playing my guitar
Now everything I got
Is in the backseat of my car
I got the Butte Fire Blues
I got the Butte Fire Blues
Ain't nothin' been the same since the fire came rolling through

Got no FEMA Trailer
Got no money for the rent
I'm out here in the cold and rain
Living in a tent
I got the Butte Fire Blues
I got the Butte Fire Blues
Ain't nothin' been the same since
the fire came rolling through

Connie Collins

43

Evacuate

Shannon Jewel

The call to evacuate came in the wee hours on 9/11/15.
I thought I was well prepared for an emergency.
Water—check. Food rations—check.
When the flames were out and evacuation orders lifted,
the fire chief escorted me up the hill past smoldering stumps
in acres of ash. I was fortunate to have a roof over my head.
It was time to sleep but sleep didn't come. The indoor air was
a smoky haze that made my eyes burn and my chest tight.
I could barely breathe. I lay awake until the sun came up
an eerie orange hue.
The usual morning songbirds did not sing,
I was not prepared for the feelings that followed the fire.

Don Seeman

Out of the Fire
Denella Kimura

Found objects define the woman's gifts
    by their handy usefulness:
The butcher knife slices a rump roast,
the chopping knife minces garlic, onions and celery
the seven-tined fork tosses vegetables for salad
    her hands busy cooking nutritious meals
        for children
            husband
                friends.
Here the tools of the seamstress lie broken:
    the bobbins and embroidery scissors,
        gears and hinges from a sewing machine
Charred, rusted, bleak reminders
That a woman lived here in this old house
    where smoke still spins in the whirlwind
Even as Vulcan, god of the firestorm
    rises like a spirit
        reborn from the ashes
So we renew our hope that the woman's gifts were not lost,
    but treasured in the hearts of those loved.
Rise up, O Phoenix, from the blackened hills,
    lift the weight of loss from our hearts
        leaving only loving memories
            purified in golden tears.

Kent Lambert

Dragon Breath
Anne Cook

45 Years of My Words Away
Conrad Levasseur

So how do I write about something
that took 45 years of my words & art away?

Journals, articles, poems, drawings, paintings, manuscripts,
travel sketches, a library & research files, every letter
and post card from the three kids, Margaret, family, friends.

A goldrush mine of memory
that I wanted to dig into in retirement
to shovel, rake, sift, pan and separate
all the nuggets from the general debris.

After the fire
only the rammed earth adobe walls
still standing.

Everything else melted or
bent or pulverized into
soft, fine ash.

Even the half dozen
cords of wood
in the open field
that were chain sawed, split, stacked
neatly in geometric rows

patiently waiting through
the drought-dried summer simmering heat
to perform their duty
in the Vermont Casting wood stove

as soon as the first beautiful
silver frost wolves of winter
came running down
the slopes
of the Sierra

now sit
but a handful
of delicate
fine ash.

Ty Childress

The power of the flame
to totally dissolve
a refrigerator,
liquify glass
and melt machines.

All those hundreds of hours
spent getting beyond clearance
with the undergrowth
inching my way through
oak, manzanita, cedar, pine,
miners' misery, poison oak, star thistle

Now beyond – beyond clearance.

Every nook, valley, slope, hill
creek, drainage on the acreage

nakedly exposed
beyond all my years
of intimacy with them.

There were some ghost books
that lay on their backs,
binders spread open,
at a hundred and eighty degrees

an accordion of pages
eerily beckoning
to be picked up
and played
one last time

collapsing with their final breath
when delicately touched
by a finger cautiously seeking
that final secretive tale.

Somehow family history
still clung to the walls
reminding me of archeological sites
I visited around the world.

Kent Lambert

I first thought
of leaving the walls
to be buried
by moss, lichens, vines

a new forest monument
to my family living
for a short period together
at the edge of the grid

my mother's ashes
spread around the property
weaving a genetic thread
from the Old World to the New.

47

When Margaret and I drove back the first time
and got out of the car, both of us thought
one of us whispered, *The silence — it's so quiet here.*

Unimaginably quiet
beyond the cherished silence
that had nurtured us
all these years.

No tracks of squirrel, skunk, raccoon, bear, coyote,
mountain lion, wild turkey, wild pig, dog, cat.

No bird songs.

One set — one set
out of dozens before
of deer tracks
clearly imprinted
in the ash-sealed road.

Of course,
the walls did have to come down
the land did have to be cleared

leaving an open, empty field.

A haunted forest?

Or, a fresh, new
field of dreams?

Yet to be written.

Gordon Long

John Slot

One Year Ago
Gayle Lorraine

02.18.16
pausing
pondering
busy thinking and wondering
wandering in my mind
I take momentary vacations to the future
try to design a path
or sit and transport back to a lost present moment
either way I go leaves me here in the same place
still paused and wondering

02.25.16
there is a mirror
where is my face?
where have I gone?
no place
no place
there is a room
with two chests and a bed
storage cubes in a cupboard
two doors slide open a closet
outside is a place
trees, hills, sky and grass
neighbors both sides
one says hello
one is not there
unoccupied domicile
I travel in circles
as I move in a straight line
I'm amoeba in box without edges defined
lines on a paper
lines on my face
searching and seeking
my place
my place

02.25.16
there are many things to be aware of
but future worry is not one
fate may be linked with destiny
or not
no future is possible
without the errant wind to blow one forward

Kent Lambert

Little White Cup
M.J. Mallery

Oh, my goodness!
Before the fire I held hot chocolate, marshmallows swirled
about my rim and gave the kids foamy mustaches.
Sometimes my chicken soup put smiles on their
measle-marked faces.

What am I to do now?
Take up knitting? Maybe I'll make a shawl for Aunt Ida.
Train for the Olympics? I'm too fragile for pole vaulting.
Perhaps I'll dabble in politics and run for Congress.
Maybe I'll become President!

Oh no! A hand is tossing me into the trash.
Help, I'm stuck. I can't move.
Thanks, Poet, for rescuing me from oblivion.

Gordon Long

The World on Fire
Chrys Mollett

We caringly tended
our little piece of the ancient fire
Welcoming its bright warmth on chilly nights
Preparing candlesticks & tablecloths
We cooked bread & beans
for our daily fare.

Then it came
like a thief in the night
We watched in awe of its power
Then we ran.
Our animals ran.
Some have been found
Many were burned.
I still imagine their fits & fears
and the brave horror of their sacrifice.
But still it grew.
Wanton, wilder, hungrier.
Few could outrun it moving 70 feet a minute,
taking everything.

Briefly contained nations
masses of land, forest, waters
The families, the single men & women holed up in shacks & cabins.
My God, the treasures: photographs, pianos!
The crawling, grazing, flying things
whose home it was,
Singed and barren.
Now growing a new green again
Their song still sweeps the sky.

Woodlings
Suzanne Murphy

It was a possibility to listen
to human tribes, once upon a time
when winter storms gusted
and spring balming breezes whispered
along the limbs of redwoods and cedars.

Hikers trailed along sharp-edged schist
and moss-shouldered rocks,
feet stirred up pine scents on forest walks,
faces lifted to the sun dapple above
and souls to a tree's blessings.

When woodland sentinels are felled
by firestorm or cultivators' scars,
both those thieves who steal green majesty,
grey ash and sawdust pepper the air
to drive away communities and creatures

The roar of dry silence — a desert —
faeries and owls alike fled refuges
but not forever. Come again watery courses
to lay down nurseries of seedlings
that bide their own growing time

Secreted abundance below sleeping earth
no one sees the slow way roots force
themselves into the labor of reclamation,
save for the sun that rises each day and
celebrates the return of air so sweet to breathe

Rising in a generation clothed in new raiment
trees, river waters, golden grasses, forest denizens
make of the world a place for wonderment.
Caution, though — this time humans step softly
and listen to the voices of the forest.

Gordon Long

When the Music Stopped
Cynthia Restivo

Doris and her daughter Jill packed their Subaru with their dogs, goats, and enough clothes for a few days and drove out of the smoke. They stayed with friends in Stockton for more than a week hearing conflicting reports. People who stayed behind messaged her, "Your house is still there," or "I went by and no, sorry your house is gone. That whole area got wiped out, yesterday," or "It's there. I saw it, just this morning." Doris couldn't get off the roller coaster of uncertainty. As soon as they opened the roads, she queued with others from the community who needed to know — either way.

She drove into a scarred scene. Her road, formerly bustling with comings and goings of busy lives, now deserted. Only blackened matchstick trees stood sentinel, witnessing her tears flow as she turned onto the long gravel driveway. Halfway up she stopped the car and got out, knowing. An acrid smell filled her nostrils. Her footsteps replaced the silence. At the end of the driveway, she looked out at empty space. No porch, no stairs or railing, no walls or door, no windows or roof – no house. Where had it gone? Oh, she knew it had burned, but where did it go? Where did all the rooms go? And the porch? How was it possible? All that, reduced to the small pile of rubble before her? The iron and tiles, porcelain and steel, wood and glass, paper and aluminum, plastic and stone, tin and ceramics, rubber and Formica, the brass and wire — where did it all go?

Doris stood where her house had once existed. Seeing a couple of blackened Corningware bowls still stacked where the kitchen had been, she reached over to retrieve them from the ashes, but with the touch of her finger, they disintegrated. She pulled back her hand in horror. She searched the black rubble, careful not to step on charred remains. When she got to her daughter's room, she stopped and sank to the ground. She reached into the ashes to retrieve a metal clarinet. How could she have forgotten this? It had been with the family for such a long time. She rocked back and forth, cradling it, tears moistening her cheeks.

She remembered.

Her Grandpa's mustached lips embraced the clarinet's mouthpiece. His playing made everything swing. When Grandpa played tunes, nobody could sit still. From the kitchen they could hear Grandma swing with the clatter of pots and pans — the washing of vegetables, the stirring of spoons and the cutting of knives, everything in rhythm to Grandpa's playing. And it wasn't long before Grandma, in the doorway of the living room, swayed from side to side. She reached over and snatched up Doris and her brother Will, and the three of them danced, twisting and turning, swirling and twirling, as each passed one to the other. Grandma danced as if Grandpa's music spun an invisible thread, leading Grandma around the living room dance floor. Then Grandma threw her head back and laughed as she sashayed back to the kitchen to pick up her cooking in rhythm.

Doris remembered.

Her brother bit the mouthpiece grudgingly to squeak his way through the band music. By the time Will was old enough for the school band, Grandpa had throat cancer and could no longer play his clarinet, so he gave it to her brother. Will wanted to play the trumpet and fussed, "Grandpa's clarinet is too old. It's not even wooden like they have nowadays. The band teacher said metal clarinets are too old and have a terrible sound." But Doris knew better. She wanted to play Grandpa's clarinet, but she wouldn't be in the school band for two years. She didn't understand why it was given to Will just because he was in the school

band first. He neglected the clarinet, buried it under dirty clothes on the floor of his room, or used it as a sword to fight Doris back when she dared to enter. On the rare occasions when Will actually practiced, the clarinet squeaked, screeched, and squealed.

She remembered.

Her daughter wrapped her sweet lips around the clarinet's mouthpiece for her first concert. When the girl was old enough for the school band, Doris asked her brother if he still had Grandpa's clarinet. She had to remind him it was a metal clarinet and its case had snakeskin on the outside and maroon velvet on the inside. Will thought he did remember, but kept forgetting to look for it. So in September 2014, Doris went to visit Will and search through boxes neatly stacked in his garage. She found the snakeskin case. It had a shoelace tied to one end to make up for a broken latch. But when she opened the case, Grandpa's clarinet wasn't there. She tore open the next box and let the contents spill onto the floor. One box after another, she threw stuff to the side searching for the clarinet. Why hadn't Will put it back in its case?

When she was nearing the end of the boxes, she found it, standing upright, the mouthpiece poking above the other contents of the box. The reed was broken and the bell was dented, but finally she held it. Doris threw Will's things back in the boxes and left.

Doris took the clarinet to a repair shop, where the owner changed the pads, smoothed out the dents and dings, and gave her new reeds. She presented her daughter with the clarinet and told her it had beautiful music locked inside. Jill asked, "How can I hear it?"

"Practice," answered Doris. Jill took the clarinet into her room and squeaked out 'Hot Cross Buns.' Most days her daughter did practice, and when it came time for the spring concert, Jill was given a solo. She practiced at every opportunity in the weeks leading up to the concert. On the afternoon of the concert, after Jill dressed in a black skirt and white blouse, she wanted to practice the program one more time before they left. Doris sat down on the living room floor and looked up, as her daughter wrapped her sweet lips around the clarinet's mouthpiece. She closed her eyes and heard her grandfather's music in the notes her daughter played. Then she smiled, knowing that one day her daughter would swing like Grandpa.

Now sitting on the blackened earth, Doris cradled the clarinet's skeleton forever silenced by the fire. She fingered the keys permanently fused shut and touched a hole in the wall of the bell. The mouthpiece—melted in the heat of the flames—left a jagged end to the family clarinet.

Gordon Long

Brent Duffin

Jetta

Mark Russell

Okay, so on Thursday morning at 7 a.m. I go to breakfast with Rick Schaad down at Perkos, and they're closed for ADA remodeling, so we head out to Thomi's in south Jackson, but the power is out there, so we head to Mel's, full of evacuees, but open.

After breakfast I head home and see that the plume of smoke from the canyon is looking mighty close to my house. I decide that it might be prudent to gather up some stuff and put it in the trailer just in case, but the truck has the topper on it and the fifth wheel hitch isn't installed. No worry. I go to start the truck and the battery is completely dead, so I have to maneuver the Jetta close enough where I can jump-start the truck. I move the truck to the garage, leave it running while I lift the topper off, pull it out of the garage to install the hitch and for some reason turn the truck off, and it won't start again.

At the same time I'm noticing very thick black and orange smoke arching right over the top of the house, and I can see the smoke boiling through the trees. I check my phone for evacuation updates, and my phone dies. (To be honest, I had been putting off getting a new phone after the on/off switch quit working a few months ago.) The only way I can restart the phone is to plug it in, but the power is off, so I have to use the car charger, but the Jetta's ACC port doesn't work unless the engine is running, so I have to start the Jetta and leave it running to reboot the phone, which takes about five minutes.

Still calm, I start installing the fifth wheel hitch on the truck, an easy ten-minute, two-person job, but a difficult hour-long one-person job involving multiple socket wrenches and a roll of duct tape. All the while I'm watching the smoke get thicker, checking the Cal Fire website for evacuation updates, and having to start the Jetta and reboot the phone every time.

I finally get the hitch installed, check the evac update and see that I'm being ordered out immediately on a mandatory evacuation. Now I'm getting a little bit stressed. I go back into the house and am able to stuff two of the cats, Trooper and Little Shit, into cat carriers with only a few wounds, but the third cat, Floozie, is nowhere to be found. I spill some food into her dish and start hauling the heirlooms and photos out to the truck.

Now there is a constant din of aircraft overhead, helicopters and bombers, and a huge DC10 VLAT comes skimming over at what seems like treetop level. It's starting to feel like a war zone, and I'm getting frantic when I hear fire trucks coming down Timber Ridge Road to force evacuations. I feel like I probably need to move along. I move the Jetta over to the truck and jump-start it, then drive the truck down to the shed to hitch up the trailer. That requires backing down a short but narrow and steep dirt ramp to the shed, which would make it harder to jump the truck again if I had to. I can hear the firemen at the neighbors' banging on the door. Fortunately, I'm able to get the trailer hitched in record time, and I pull out of the shed without killing the engine.

I hear the fire trucks coming back up the road now and remember the two cats in carriers still sitting in the kitchen, so I run back up to the house, grab my cats, the phone and charger out of the Jetta (which is still running), and dash back down to the truck. The growling cats go into the trailer, and I jump into the truck, put it in gear and pull out onto the one-lane road in front of two fire trucks coming up the hill. It's a fairly steep gravel climb up to Tabeaud Road from my driveway, and I keep it in fourth gear low so I don't kill the engine and make it to the road in front of the fire trucks. I don't know what would have happened if I had stalled; the fire fighters surely would have helped me, but I have visions of being shoved off the road into the brush as they go by.

A steady stream of cars, all loaded to the gunwales with crap and looking like the Joads, headed out toward 88. A dozen police cars (Oakland? Napa? Lodi?) and five fire trucks, sirens screaming and lights flashing, blow by me in the other direction. Heading east up the hill, there's a bumper-to-bumper traffic jam at 88. The police are turning back frantic drivers who are unsuccessfully trying to get onto Tabeaud Road and to their homes in Pine Acres to save what they can. In the meantime, Grace is racing up from Stockton but arrives too late, I call her and we meet at Rick and Denise Schaad's house. They have no power or water but at least are not in the evacuation zone. We all decide to tow the trailers down to Jackson and set up a refugee camp behind Safeway, where we can hook into power and have restroom access at Denise's Bodies-N-Balance studio.

We spend the rest of the day at loose ends, watching the smoke and aerial attacks in the distance, and a constant string of screaming fire trucks, bulldozers on flatbeds, and PG&E equipment moving on the highway below. When evening comes, Grace drives back to Stockton, and I bed down with the cats in our little refugee camp. The southern sky glows bright orange from the flames, and I'm hoping that the house is OK, but I have no way of knowing for sure.

That was Thursday. Friday is a new phone and truck battery, a shower at the Foothill Conservancy office in Jackson, and finally a move from the Safeway camp to the most gracious Giles and Shirley Turner's home in Sutter Creek. From our fabulous friends in Amador County, we have had at least a dozen offers of refuge.

Today, Saturday, is a waiting game, and who knows how it will turn out. With the incredible efforts being made by Cal Fire, plus all the local, California, and national mutual support emergency agencies, and, of course, all of the organizations and individuals locally who are opening their businesses, homes and hearts to their neighbors, I know that everything that can be done is being done, regardless of the outcome. It is what it is, and I am okay with that.

But I still can't remember for the life of me if I turned the Jetta off.

Gordon Long

Gordon Long

Meandering
Selma Sattin

Cows in the rolling pasture
Grunch, munch, slunch
Tossing salad bunch by bunch.

Cows by the curvy creek
Lap, slap, slurp
Loudly mooing bubbly burps.

Cows 'neath the lonesome oak
Yawn, nod, sigh
Watchful with a dreamy eye.

Cows along a narrow path
Lumbering, lowing
Heading home.

Selma Sattin

What Time Is It?
by Ann Seely

I have no idea what time it was when the sheriff's vehicle drove down Gold Strike Road and announced through a bullhorn to evacuate. We don't check our watches. I run to the back yard and turn on the sprinklers. We put the dogs, the cat, the kids, the arguing women, and everything else in the car and we go, leaving the front door unlocked, as instructed.

This is our Ground Zero.

I have never had to leave a home this way. I never looked back. I knew what was behind us, a huge black cloud of smoke bearing down on us with all its might.

Somewhere during those five days, we learned:

Our neighbor's ranch house had burned down. He had gotten a special escort so he could get his Chaplain's uniform. When he got to the top of the hill, everything was gone. He said he did not know anything about our house because the smoke had been too thick.

Sender's Market had burned down, but I didn't believe it. Finally I saw Caroline's pictures posted on Facebook as proof that the market was still there.

Even if you buy a harness and leash, your cat will still lie down in the grass and not take a walk.

The priceless paintings your great-uncle painted can get damaged though you try your best to keep them safe.

When you pack up and go home to see if your house is still there, you still might not know what happened to it for another five days. Our other-side neighbor was a contractor from San Francisco. He drove from San Francisco in his Luminalt truck, sneaked through the CHP barricades, and sent us a cellphone picture of our house. Both our houses were still standing. CHP would not let us through for another week.

If your husband has a job interview, he can drive through the Sender's property on a dirt road, and CDF firefighters will let him pass because he needs to get his suit and tie out of the house. No questions asked.

Your ranch is close to the road, so maybe, just maybe, a heavy CDF fire truck might be able to get up your steep driveway and save your house and your neighbor's houses. Might damage the concrete a bit, but that's okay.

If you are strong and own a tractor, you can plough a firebreak and save a whole town, almost all by yourself.

When you take your kids on a much-needed vacation to Washington, D.C. after a fire like that, chances are you'll wake up with your face paralyzed and have to get a cab to the hospital. The doctor said I had Bell's palsy. Caused by a mystery virus. Or stress. Or nerve compression. Or all three.

One morning I drove to Treat's General Store in San Andreas and parked in the lot. I looked through the fence at the ridge and imagined the ridge on fire, spewing black clouds of smoke. But there was only green grass, bright sun and blue sky. There's a dent in my home's roof and in our front yard stands an ash tree, its bare arms reaching to the sky in supplication.

Wayne Carlson

Wayne Carlson

Wayne Carlson

Butte Fire Memoir: The Beginning

Gail Stark

June 1, 2016

It was Wednesday, September 9th, and we were at home busy with preparations for a three-day family reunion to celebrate my husband's eightieth birthday when we heard about a fire across the Mokelumne River near the city of Jackson. It caught our attention but raised no alarms, so we continued making arrangements for a full program of games and parties for the three generations flying in from other states. However, that evening we could see smoke in the sky, and a friend's cousin, a firefighter from the Bay Area, told us, "I don't like the looks of that. I'm going back, get my stuff, and then I'm out of here!" We thought he was over-reacting.

By the next morning, the situation had become threatening. We faced a dilemma: do we cancel the entire weekend after months of planning? Our daughter-in-law Susan was driving to Mountain Ranch with her daughter in a truck loaded with boxes of decorations and masses of fresh flowers for the celebration. Should we call and tell her not to come? And that, as I look back, was the beginning of the downward spiral that still surrounds and permeates our daily lives and our dark-of-night thoughts. We called Susan. She said they were coming anyway.

When Susan and Katie arrived, they told us they had watched the sky in disbelief all the way to Mountain Ranch. We didn't know what action to take. The sky grew ever darker as the minutes passed. An unearthly light illuminated the towering pines. Should we stay? Should we go? Evacuate, an almost incomprehensible thought.

How could we leave our twenty-two acres of lush, towering, protecting pines, fir, and cedar? Leave the two hundred-year-old oaks that housed the native birds and fed the squirrels and deer their bountiful acorns every fall? Leave the home we had so lovingly built and enhanced for over forty years? Leave a place that harbored the heart and soul of four generations of our family?

When warm, blackened oak leaves three inches in diameter fell from the sky, when the sun was obscured by smoke and the sky turned a menacing black, we made the decision. Fueled by a sense of fear, growing urgency and sadness, the four of us began loading our daily lives and family history, mostly precious, some not so precious—just necessary—into our vehicles. Katie, at twenty-one years, gathered with quiet purpose and grace my jewelry and personal items without letting her own emotions interfere with her somber mission.

And what did I do? I think I emptied the safe. I know I was in motion, making immediate decisions about what to take and what to leave. However, as I write I find a blank until my SUV held, shivering in the back, our huge white Anatolian goat guard dog and the orange Manx loudly protesting being crammed into an ill-fitting cat carrier.

No authority personnel told us to evacuate, so we determined on our own to take what we could carry of our lives in a car, a truck, and an SUV. When we drove out the driveway, we couldn't look back for that "one last image" because we needed all our driving skill and composure as we entered a situation that was beyond weird.

We joined a non-stop chain of people and animals in vehicles of every description, age, and condition moving slowly in single file, headlights on, down the only road leading away. Canopied by the now-black sky that seeped a diabolical light we, escapees and mourners, put our sadness and grief on hold. We buried them somewhere deep only to surface later as confusion, forgetfulness, quick temper, unexplainable fatigue, high blood pressure, anxiety and insomnia.

Only thirty-six hours after the Butte fire sparked miles and miles away, our neighborhood fled before its incendiary onslaught.

Within half an hour, believing we were safe, our family caravan lined up at our son Hy's small house. We weren't safe though, and the very next day we were forced to evacuate again. This time we descended upon Susan and Michael's house in Walnut Creek. It was there that the birthday party guests from out of state converged. We tried to have a jolly celebration, but not knowing if our home and property were consumed by flames kept us mostly distracted.

As the weekend wound down, the four generations bade their farewells and headed home. My husband Bill and I returned to Hy's house. For several days, we had no information, and all roads to the fire area were blocked. Nine days after we had fled the flames, our neighbor called in the morning to tell us that the blockade on West Murray Creek had finally been lifted. At last we could see for ourselves what had happened to our home.

John Slot

Butte Fire Memoir: The Middle
June 3, 2016

West Murray Creek Road is a long, arduous, poorly-maintained road from San Andreas that ends at Whiskey Slide Road, the corner of our property. It winds up the side of a mountain to what had once been a fire lookout station and then heads downhill toward Mountain Ranch. With long driveways branching off West Murray Creek Road, numerous secluded homesites enjoyed privacy and spectacular views the trees and elevation provided all year, every year.

We quickly started off up the road to Mountain Ranch to find out what had happened to our property and neighborhood. Having heard sobering descriptions from others, we felt we were mentally prepared. Nothing, nothing could have prepared us for the magnitude of devastation we witnessed driving from San Andreas to the Lookout and back down to our corner. Only the black skeletal remains of pine, oak, maple, fir and madrone greeted us. Not a leaf or a needle, not even a blade of grass, remained. Bare darkened earth exposed what were once private roads now meandering across dead land to vanished homes. From canyon and gully to ridge tops, the disaster rose and fell and rose again.

As we approached our corner, we were hopeful but apprehensive that we would only find ruins like the ones we were driving past. When we reached our driveway, our house appeared exactly as we had left it. Two pines and two liquid ambers near the front of the house stood as well, along with an old grandfather oak in the back. Our enormous relief quickly turned to dismay as we looked up the driveway toward the well house. It was gone. Nothing remained except the metal corrugated roofing material lying on the ground and covering the footprint of the structure. There were no charred pieces of wall wood or beams. The building had vaporized, the fire had been so hot. If the pump and pressure tank had also been destroyed, we had no water.

While the well house could be replaced, that wasn't true for the remainder of our twenty-two acres. We stared in sickened disbelief at every once-living thing that was either badly burned or burned beyond recognition. Our land, the home of deer and fox, squirrels and turkeys, blue jays and woodpeckers, had been annihilated. The homes of bees, ants, worms, and more life forms than I ever knew lived there were gone. Nothing but tall black sticks and blackened earth remained. Again, not one single pine needle or blade of grass could be seen, all vaporized.

Gordon Long

70

In the weeks and months that followed, and even now, a difficulty arose for those of us whose houses were spared but whose land had burned beyond recognition. We found it impossible to explain our profound grief, our sense of loss to those whose homes had burned to the ground. "But you still have your house," they told us. There were hundreds who had lost everything. "No," we say, "please, please, try to understand. You see, we do have our houses, but we have lost our homes. More than the buildings, our homes encompassed the land, the trees, and the wildlife that shared that particular piece of earth with us."

We have lost our daily images. We have lost what has been our refuge, our safety and support. It all is forever compromised, never to share its many life-giving and life-sustaining properties, never to whisper in the breeze or toss violently in a winter storm. Never again will it be a shelter for litters of fox kits, hideouts for young children's first club, or a place to show them the intricacies and layers of the life it fostered. We who lost our home, but retained our house, chose the foothills precisely for the variety and wonder of their intrinsic beauty. We wanted — needed — to have our spirits interact with all the life present in the natural world. Yes, we have our houses, but we ache and hold a deep longing because our spirits have nowhere to go.

Kent Lambert

Maria Camillo

2015 Butte Fire Legacy

Pru Starr

my jeweler friend no longer works
a blobmelt inventory breaks her heart
incomprehensible to those who weren't evacuated

transform an ugly story
twenty minutes before the house burns down
only rubble survives its raw beauty

cherry-pick the jewelry box when my brain says
I'm coming back
who wears melted gold around her neck
when its clasp no longer opens?

how does a dish cope in a new shape
will the teacup hang without its handle

rusty hacksaw suspends in burnt wood
where is the bed when only twisted box springs remain?

remember heat-snapped shards in gray ash dirt
water turns to mud where once there was a garden

Kent Lambert

Butte Fire September 2015

Charleen Tyson

We are just six women, having fun on holiday in Ashland, until we find out there is a huge wildfire approaching our homes in Calaveras County, a six-hour drive away. We head home only to be evacuated.

We are lucky, the wind changed just before getting to West Point; so many are not so lucky. I know only one family who was burned out. Lynn Keever and Charlie Campbell are jewelers. Crystal Geometrics is their business, and along with Lynn's son, James Keever, they make many of their pieces using dichroic glass. Even if you already know the beautiful creation that is dichroic glass, you'll like what wikipedia tells us about it, "Multiple ultra-thin layers of different metals (such as gold or silver); oxides of such metals as titanium, chromium, aluminum, zirconium, or magnesium, or silica are vaporized by an electron beam in a vacuum chamber." With all that going on, it better be something good, and it is. Oh, yeah.

Thoughts of all that beautiful glass ruined by the wildfire and lost as a medium for jewelry rankles me. Surely there must be some other way to use it. I ask Lynn if she has thought of maybe a "beauty out of devastation" sort of thing, but she says she just isn't going back there. She tells me that if I want to, I can go collect whatever might be usable.

My husband and I see what it is that Lynn did not want to see. Their house is mostly ash. The ceiling and roof have collapsed onto the bottom floor, covering everything in a thick layer of ash, wet from the recent rain, and melted asphalt shingles. We start poking around in what had been the workroom, identified by the kilns, still standing.

Metal containers hold colored glass rods like wilted bouquets on a window ledge. A four-inch optical glass "diamond" has shattered inside but retained its overall shape. Saws, glass cutters, jeweler's tools, and unidentifiable pieces of metal are crusted black, some with the beautiful glass melted onto them. Many of the glass jewelry pieces that Lynn and Charlie had already created are bent like Dali clocks or intruded upon by the odd screw or nail.

Thin sheets of glass had been arranged in stacks, and now fused, will stay stacked forever; they form amorphous layered shapes that gleam in the sun. What can I do with this stuff? I'll worry about that later. It's too beautiful just as it is to not be given a second chance.

We scrub, soak, pick at, sand, and admire in the sun the booty we have collected. Ash had melted into some of the glass. Asphalt coated, splattered or welded other pieces together.

Now, what to do with all this grand stuff. Perhaps outline the wood grain of a manzanita stump with narrow strips of the glass. Maybe a few of those lovely, almost flat shards or instead a spray of those wiggly colored glass rods. How about mobiles that hang in the sun to be reminded of the glory that is dichroic glass, to remember what this has meant for me, bringing something beautiful out of something so bad.

Gordon Long

Maria Camillo

Kent Lambert

Home
Caitlin M. Wilbur

I know in my bones how blessed we are, but I wake from dreams of our bodies tangled in the blankets of our first bed. The soft morning light shyly makes its way into our room as Lucy's whiskers tickle my face. In these dreams I can smell freshly ground coffee beans and the cedar tree outside our bathroom window. I can hear the rhythmic chopping of zucchini from our summer garden, the sizzling of bacon in a well-loved cast iron skillet.

I miss wiping down the counter tops and mopping our dusty floors. I miss singing as I worked, windows flung open to a cool mountain breeze. Have you ever noticed the sound the wind makes through an ocean of pines? I'd often sit barefoot on the edge of the porch with my eyes closed to listen.

In my dreams I feel the dirt beneath my fingernails, a clothespin held awkwardly between my lips as my hands fight to keep a wet sheet from the ground. I see the dogs chasing each other through the lupines in the clearing and around my favorite ancient oak. The cat lounges lazily in a windowsill. In these dreams I hear my husband sink an ax into a large wood round. Over and over again. I feel the perfect lengths in my gloved hands as we stack the chopped wood away for winter's warmth. And oh, how I can see the stars. You've never seen stars so bright. Undisturbed by city lights, some nights I swear, we could touch them.

At least the stars remain.

Gordon Long

76

Wayne Carlson

I Didn't Know

Caitlin M. Wilbur

I started writing again the day before my house burned to the ground. That was one week ago. I mentioned something about fire being cleansing, but that was before it ever reached anyone I love. I didn't think it would come for us, but it did. And when it did, it came fast and strong. I don't have words for the images I carry with me into the wee hours of the morning, only setting them down so I can close my eyes. I don't have words for the ache in my chest or the way our bodies swell with pride watching our neighbors labor to help one another. I have seen men and women fight to save another's home while their own still smolders. I have seen strangers embrace and old friends offer words of comfort and the use of their own hands.

Tonight I sort through what few pieces of clothing we took with us. The sweet smell of burnt pine lingers on a favorite sweater. I sit on the end of the bed in this small room cradling my head in my hands, remembering the hurried hours before our home went up in flames. I paced the floors then, forsaking housework in order to watch out the windows. The ash and blackened oak leaves fell all around, and I talked myself out of being scared. *Don't be silly. It couldn't move that fast*. But those canyons. Those trees. The dry, dry grass. *They'll tell us if we need to go*. Funny how I can now recall that every inch of my body was on edge. My brow furrowed. My gut questioned my reason. Instead of packing, I picked tomatoes.

As the sky turned orange and the ash fell more furiously, I spoke with my neighbor, and our eyes said what our mouths could not. Maybe we should get ready to go. The person on the hotline said we should just be prepared. He didn't sound concerned. I'll shower. Wait for my husband. I should grab the box on the top shelf of the closet. Where's my engagement ring anyway?

Jack called. He sounded excited and not yet worried for our land. We're just being cautious, baby. Do grab the box on the top shelf of the closet. By the time he got home, the wind swirled in small circles around the yard and kicked up what I now know to be the ashes of friends' homes. The lights flickered quickly as I moved from room to room, and a foreign heat radiated through the trees behind our house. When the distant explosions first started, I almost convinced myself that my ears were playing tricks on me. But the blasts only sounded closer and more frequent. I'll never forget following our yellow Jeep out the gate, Jack motioning to drive on, signaling that I shouldn't bother to close it. The ash danced in our headlights like falling snow. As our cars melted into the river of vehicles hurrying down the mountain, I looked back over my right shoulder as flames silhouetted the ridge behind us. Alone in my car, with what little we'd thought to take precariously stacked in the back, I cried for the first time.

Ty Childress

Chamomile tea, and she

Joy Willow

steam rises still
from swan-neck spout,
teapot dream of unbroken bowls
breakfast arrested mid-sip;
chamomile quiets the nerves
of shaking hands, and she stirs
sugar with the long spoon,
spreads butter with the proper knife,
the bread, salted and broken,
dissolves on the tongue

Gordon Long

Asher Wilson

When a half dozen fire engines pulled onto their property located on the east side of Murphys Grade Road off of Canyon Drive, Kyle and Sarah Wilson thought the worst: the fire had jumped the Grade Road. As the fire engines halted, the family went outside to speak to the approaching fire fighter. Expecting to be told to evacuate, they learned instead the fire fighters were asking for help. They were lost! Three year old Asher Wilson is shown here lending his support, and was rewarded with 'Junior Fire Fighter' badges that he proudly wore (along with 'Wolverine' cap and skivvies).

Sarah Wilson

Sarah Wilson

Make It Rain

Jerry Allen Zellers
Dedicated to my dad, Scott Zellers, the bravest man I know

It was a hot, dry year in a long line of hot, dry years stretching back through the past decade, and we stood at the peak of a fierce drought. The priests of meteorology were predicting heavy rainfall for the winter, and we prayed to El Niño for salvation. I took a dive into the pool. Floating on my back, I gazed up at the sun through the fingers of a mighty oak tree.

I was on the deck, facing westward, when I caught my first glimpse of the smoke — a thin, grey column rising small but ominous over the ridge against the clear blue sky. A column thickening and turning black before my eyes, reaching from beyond the hills. I sent a text message to Dad's phone with a picture, getting Mom's response that they were on their way home, about five hours out.

Then she called. "The fire is on Butte Mountain, so as long as it's on the other side of the river we should be safe."

"It looks so close."

"If you want, you can call Cal Fire. They've probably got a lot of planes out right now, so they should know what's going on."

"Alright, I'll do that."

Butte Mountain is about ten miles northwest as the crow flies, on the other side of the river canyon dividing Calaveras from Amador County. Cal Fire confirmed what Mom had said. Taking one last look at the smoke and mounting the quad with a jump, I drove back to the house, my mind spinning like a cog seeking broken teeth.

Lunchbox, my sister Rachelle's boyfriend, arrived. He described what he saw, an isolated but burgeoning fire in the canyon spewing copious smoke, and the early stages of aircraft intervention. The sky was turning red and yellow as we spoke, with the sun falling and the smoke rising. I caught my first whiff of brimstone, carried on a bitter and merciless wind.

The power went out. I called Mom again, and she told me the fire had jumped the river. As the last rays of the sun stretched futilely over the land, I took the quad to the hilltop again and beheld a terrible sight.

Flames were coming out of the canyon, sinuous, undulating yellow teeth devouring green earth in the shadows of the setting sun. A choral drone echoed inside my skull — dreadful, as if the flames spoke, as if they were alive.

Mom and Dad got home at a little past nine, and we shifted gears. They had seen the fire coming up the canyon as they came down the mountain. A glow emanated over the ridge, and the air was rich with the scent of carbon. Dad took the truck out on the back road, presumably to shut off the water to the forty acres, and check the status of the fire.

We shuffled and struggled to prioritize by lamp and candlelight, stampeding through the living room/kitchen chaotically like servers in a restaurant. Mom suddenly stopped, smiled,

Fire Drop Plane
Don Seeman

and pointed at something.

A praying mantis was meditating on the couch, still and chill. Mom gazed at it with unabashed wonder, as if, for a moment, everything she and Dad had worked for over the past thirty years wasn't in the path of destruction. It was a snapshot of hope in a montage of futility.

I tried to catch the four cats, starting with Runt, the oldest and most docile. Mom brought Mr. Brown Pants, one of the two baby goats, from the upper pasture.

I grabbed my guitar and two boxes packed with Buddhist texts I had acquired working for a non-profit Tibetan book bindery. I gathered enough clothing and hygienic products to last a week or so.

Dad had pulled the truck up next to the gate of the horses' pasture and hitched up the trailer. Mom and I hauled the unwieldy cage with the cats from the front yard, stumbling and cursing with them all the way. I returned to the house to finish packing as Mom helped Dad with the horses. A few minutes later, Rachelle, Lunchbox, and I lined up with our cars behind the trailer.

"We'll meet at Raley's!" Mom shouted, driving the truck loaded down with dogs in the cab, the goat and cats in the bed. There was no room for Cyclops and Baby Bee, the oldest horses, in the trailer. Separated from his fami-ly, faced with bewildering abandonment, Cyclops let out a heartbreaking scream, and my hair stood on end.

Mom led Rachelle and me down the driveway to the highway. We turned right, bypassing the fire by crossing the canyon into Amador at a higher elevation. Dad had announced his plans to stay, so he wasn't with us. He was gearing up to face the dragon, and no one could stop him. I wasn't leaving him, so I pulled over at the turnout before the canyon, turned around and drove back.

I saw Dad in the front yard with Lunchbox in the heavy rain of ashes. Dad gave me an inscrutable look as I approached. His dark blue eyes made me flinch, and his red skin, burned from decades of working outdoors, was a constant reminder of how lazy I was in comparison. His head, large and round, sat on wide shoulders, and his biceps were the size of oak tree limbs. I felt insufficient in his presence. His gaze then turned to the west, and he said, "Basically, the fire is here."

Dad commanded Lunchbox and me to hose down everything. "See that leaf pile right there?" he said to me. "Drench it." Lunchbox took the fire hose and walked around the house, spraying it down over and over again I

Ty Childress

soaked everything in sight, into the early hours of the morning.

I slept a few hours until sunrise and started in on moving dry rotted wood away from the house to the front yard and soaking it down. The sky took on a deep reddish-yellow hue as smoke grew closer and thicker, blotting out the sun. When I saw a Cal Fire plane bank sharply overhead like a fighter jet out of World War II, I imagined the pilot shouting to me, "What are you doing? Get out of there!" The air was bitter and coarse, like burnt toast. We couldn't stay.

I had no room left in my car when Dad came across the front yard with his Fender American-made sunburst Stratocaster, an electric guitar he'd bought when we were kids and all talking about forming a family band. "You got room for this?" he asked.

"I'll make room," I promised, and I did.

We departed in a convoy. I visualized the fire ripping through the house, the teakettle flying through the kitchen, and the granite floors rising and separating with the heat. I visualized the chickens jumping from the roost in flames and Cyclops and Baby Bee running through the pasture, dodging falling trees, terrified.

We took Highway 49 to the vista point at the top of the hill. I could see smoke rising in thick black columns all along the river canyon, overtaking the sky. It was surreal that part of that smoke could be from our house. We headed down the hill to our people.

We began to put the pieces together. We could now trace the fire's growth. By the end of the day on Wednesday, it had grown to 1,200 acres, and had jumped to 2,600 by 6:00 Thursday morning. By 7:00, it had broken 4,000 acres. It doubled, and then tripled, to 14,000 acres as firefighters struggled to squelch spot fires igniting constantly ahead of the blaze on bad back roads and uneven terrain.

By early afternoon, the entire town of San Andreas was evacuated. The fire had torn its way through half of Calaveras County overnight, coming to knock at the door of the county seat. Some evacuation orders were lifted shortly afterward, but the fire reached an arm southward toward Angels Camp, where many residents and their livestock had fled to the fairgrounds serving as the main evacuation center of Calaveras. Mokelumne Hill, Glencoe, West Point, and Wilseyville were all evacuated as the fire stretched east and west along the canyon, and the population of the fairgrounds park surged, with tents popping up on any available patch of grass.

Friday morning, we packed up, cleaned out, and left the camp. There were scorch marks on the land right outside of Jackson, then some more by Electra Road near Butte Mountain. I crossed the river and ascended the hill. Coming up on Mokelumne Hill, I could see into the canyon, stripped bare and ravaged. I imagined the devastation of my own home, the fangs of fire having done their work.

What do you do when the fire's coming at you?

You crank that valve, raise that nozzle, and make it rain.

Make it rain.

Gordon Long

PIECES *Vignettes*

Melding Memory Out of the Fire

Connie Strawbridge

The Pieces Traveling Exhibit Pieces Vignettes:
Melding Memory Out of the Fire

Originating in Amador County, the Butte Fire devastated several communities in Calaveras County from September 9 through containment on October 1, 2015. The seventh most destructive fire in California history ravaged over 70,000 acres and displaced thousands of people, with 549 homes and an additional 368 structures burned. The disastrous changes to the natural landscape and forested region will affect the area for generations to come. Hope is a renewable resource, and the people of the stricken communities who still struggle with doubt and uncertainty, sorrow and loss, are an amazingly resilient group. So, too, are those who persevered with them during the fire and offered continuing aid and support long after the fire took its toll.

At the center of *The Pieces Traveling Exhibit* lies the heart of the community and the strength of those whose lives changed forever when the Butte Fire threatened to defeat the soul of our Sierra Foothill region. Sponsored by the Calaveras County Arts Council, and carefully assembled by artists Robin Modlin and Anne Cook, *The Pieces Traveling Exhibit* is an array of charred and transformed art pieces grouped into montage plays of after-fire relics rescued from the ashes. This exhibit is part of a larger project, *Pieces – A Community Healing Art Project*, which also includes a memorial mosaic wall called *Pieces: An Altar for Altered Lives*. The memorial re-imagines pieces of objects into a beautiful mosaic for remembrance. This gift to the community of those who endured the Butte Fire was presented September 10, 2016, in Mountain Ranch, California.

Manzanita Writers Press hosted ten writers who contributed poems and stories in a chapbook to honor the voices of the remains, called *Pieces Vignettes: Melding Memory Out of the Fire*. The writers involved—Nitya Prema, Suzanne Murphy, Denella Kimura, Blanche Abrams, Gayle Lorraine, Monika Rose, Linda Toren, Cynthia Restivo, as well as the Pieces project coordinator and lead artist, Robin Modlin and artist Anne Cook—have composed word vignettes that are featured along with Will Mosgrove's photographs of the objects in the collection. Excerpts from these writings travel with the exhibit. A website and blog will collect and record the fire's community links, writing, stories, poetry, photography, art, graphics and more, for the public.

The Pieces Traveling Exhibit installation and the compilation of writings, *Pieces Vignettes: Melding Memory Out of the Fire*, serve to pay tribute to a community in recovery from the devastation, while it rebuilds from the ashes. *The Pieces Traveling Exhibit*, fire-transformed relics donated by those who lost their homes in the fire, is testimony to the re-creation and renewal that art gives to people seeking to put their world back together after it has been torn apart. To view this exhibit is to experience the poignancy of loss and the determination to forge a community with a renewed sense of identity. The exhibit is permanently housed at the Calaveras County Library in San Andreas.

For the Butte Fire website, tax deductible donations can go to Manzanita Writers Press directly at manzapress.com or email manzanitawp@gmail.com.

Robin Modlin

Pieces Vignettes: Melding Memory Out of the Fire

Thank you to Butte Fire residents for sacrificing cherished objects for the beauty of art, and to the communities within and outside Calaveras County that gave of themselves to help others in dire need.

The Wall is a permanent memorial located in the town of Mountain Ranch, CA.

All Photos Submitted by Anne Cook

Inheritance
Suzanne Murphy

For the longest time I took no notice
The clock rested on the mantel
Its chimes whirred in the quiet
Filigree hands advanced the day
and night, if I cared to look
I usually did not look

Not anything I would choose for myself
It had come to me from a grandmother
A shard of brightness most precious to her
the only pretty thing in her grey life
so the story went
it marked the length of her days.

The fire consumed with greed
Its flashing tongue darted and licked to death
We all fled, grabbing what was close at hand
The little mantelpiece clock abandoned
its shiny face bubbled and slipped away
Charred hands stopped at a particular time

Our return to skeletal homes, heartbreaking
to walk the spaces, once sun-filled rooms
now stinking with smoky loss
I ran my hand along the stone mantel
touched the little clock, flame-scalded
Quite ruined to the eye

At last I know why that clock came to me
a gift from wisdom and memory
Devastation has silenced its movement
but my mind sees and hears it still
marking the deepest experiences
that tick in my soul.

Will Mosgrove

Glass Endures
Linda Toren

Remade
Reformed
Reminder

Glass endures heat
born of intensity
intent

Once a vase
for gathering ephemeral beauty

Now embraced by barnacle blue
companions, assembled by fire
in a fashion both
unkind in its urgency
abstract in its creation

Remade
Reformed
Reminder

Will Mosgrove

Will Mosgrove

Second Baptism
Suzanne Murphy

Once jeweled and transparent
now clouded and twisted
A new beauty.

Once smooth and rung like a bell
now crusted and blasted
A new talisman.

Once delicate and pleasurable in use
now weighted and stamped with ash
A new testament.

Flight
Suzanne Murphy

Waves of birds appeared
sharp edges of wings knifed through air
arrowed their terror of the flames
Rolling up into the sun
blinded, burned

A long-necked bird unfolds
even its fear elegant
vanished in the smoke
Wings forward in a kind of prayer
it swept its body into escape

II
Confusion twisted the days
absence of birdsong
an unbearable roar of silence
Land scraped bare — filthy with ash
stripped of wild life
an outraged disappearance

Birds return, in mourning
hesitant, finding no place to rest
their colors look out of place here
in a landscape barren and blackened
Skeletal trees, stark in unbidden sunlight
raise useless limbs in grief

III
Now the earth offers blooms of
melted, misshapen glass
curious new forms
cold and drained of color
entrapped reflections of wings

One day, winds carry sweet fragrances
One day, waves of birds roll overhead
Again.

Kitchenware
Linda Toren

Repurposed
    for the imagination . . .

A plate waves its blue trim
    fluid in static motion

A sombrero saucer
    ruffled by a breeze

A mug
    now a paperweight
    for what is missing

Nesting bowls
    beg to be released

It is a challenge . . .

First the event
then the long life beyond-
Days, weeks, months
    unfold in fits and starts
    runs away from memories
    finally the embrace of acceptance.

Imagination wants to rest
    beyond panic, anger, grief
    the empty bowl
    the heavy spoon.

Heart wants
    to put a piece of toast
    on the plate, soup in the bowl
    coffee in the mug.

Mind decides to let them go
    go on, knowing,
    remembering
    with nothing tangible
    but regrets.

Will Mosgrove

Searching
Linda Toren

Will Mosgrove

In balance
what survives,
so little
just a piece of
rose pale porcelain.

My open palm reaches
through ash, searches
for the valuable,
invaluable.

I was on my way
to the thrift store
more than once.
Procrastination
saved me.

My doll's hand
digs amongst loss—
the melted, distorted items
more treasured than myself
the items needed for living.

All swallowed by flames
smoke, fog-thick ash.

I am an ornament of memories lost
then found—a bracelet within my grasp.

What do we hold dear?

I think perhaps
the clear air of after
when winter washes
across the wasteland
and spring casts its
green stubble amid
blackened brush and trees.

The other day
I heard someone whisper—It's not over.

Of course
loss is never over
but does achieve
some kind of grace.

Will Mosgrove

Will Mosgrove

Fire Angel
Linda Toren

Tempered by extremes
when Hell on earth
was but a moment
that began
    sunny enough
    hot enough
    windy enough.

How does one behave
when chance
coincides with calamity?

Angels stand their post,
guardians of
good against evil.

Except for the few days
when an act of God
tested the best of them.

Buddha
Nitya Prema

This broken, charred upraised hand
A statement of strong-minded survival
Remains found, reflections remind me
Of a Buddha sitting in peaceful gesture
With upraised hand of fearlessness.

Burned, wounded, fingers — gone
Silenced, worn prayer beads once fingered
Images, pieces, create thoughts, living prayers
In depth felt sorrow, active hands and hearts
Bring healing to lands, people and community

From the Ashes
Gayle Lorraine

The Butte Fire came
uninvited to dinner
and furiously fed on
fuel leftover from
15 decades of fire suppression
Came in bellowing
sulfur yellow smoke
I saw its reflection
in crimson clouds
The frenzied feeding
such a terrible freeing
I admit:
I know its longing hunger
I know its desire
for radical change

Was it a sinister beast
or a transforming
goddess
providing a fresh start for the anima soul
of the human heart?

It shook up the people
They are trembling still

I am floating
I am falling
Catch me
Buoy me

I am lighter than air
I am heavy stone
melted silver blown glass
incinerated woods
twisted metal
I am fiber and clay

I am a woman coming out of the ashes
Creation at my fingertips

Will Mosgrove

Displaced

Anne Cook

Little bear cub
Displaced
Chance survival
Collected by its owner
Given over to artists
Creating art from ashes
To memorialize a disaster

Little bear cub
Covered in ash
Hind-section gone
Insides exposed
Itchy shards adhered
Now a receptacle
No longer collectible

Little bear cub
Looking for answers
Natural surroundings
Unrecognizable
Sterilized Earth
Not able to sustain life
In the way she knew it

Little bear cub
Displaced and adrift
Perched on what?
With three legs?
Is it strong enough?
Will my owners rebuild?
Where are they now?

Little bear cub
Needs answers to questions
Who will save me?
The government?
But which agency?
Drowning in a sea of bureaucracy
Displaced, still

Will Mosgrove

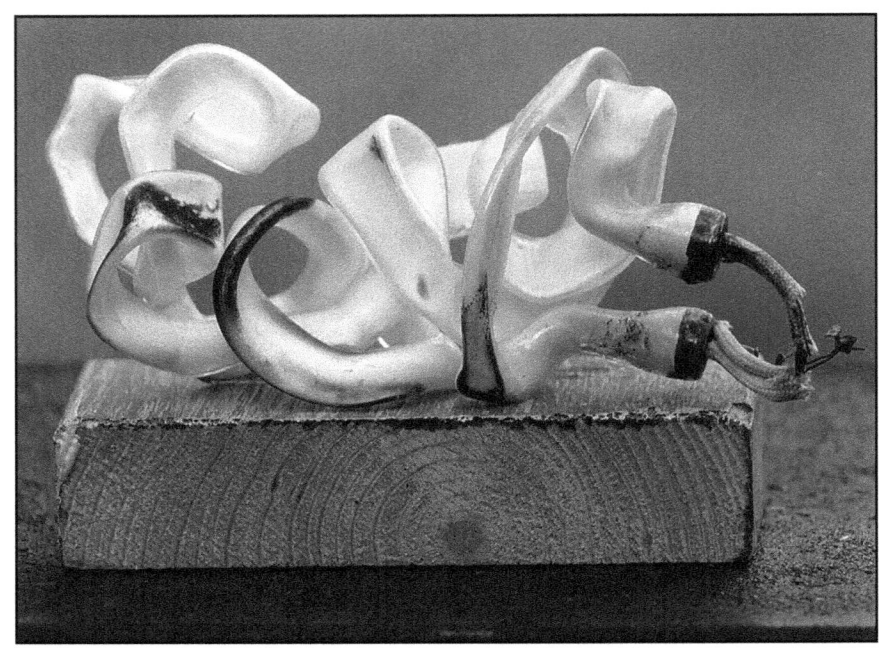

Will Mosgrove

"There will always be light," she thought, "even in my darkest times."

Light
Robin Modlin

The lights went out one night before it came. It was a windstorm that rattled the house and pulled the wires down. "No light, no precious light," she thought. How important it is to be wired, to have energy and power come to your house. It was then that she recognized a new appreciation for all of her comforts.

And then again the lights went out. A fire storm left its wake. This time the wires were not only blown from the poles but now they were burned to nothing. They were left as snaky strings in the dirt unrecognizable for the important role they played in her life. All around what was left after the fire, wild in its fury, was rubble, debris, barely any tokens of memory. One object stood out, it called to her with its twisted new form. It had changed but was recognizable. The remnants of a light bulb, strange in how it had transformed, laid at her feet. It could no longer offer the light in the night as similar bulbs had in a side lamp by her bed. The lamp was her comfort when she awoke lonely, turning it on to read. Now this twisted form no longer able to be switched on was what was left. Appreciation again arose in her mind.

She lifted the crumpled bulb in her hand as a reminder of power, so much power; the power of the fire that changed so many lives; the power of technology that transformed our culture; the power of light physical or spiritual that brightens the darkness. That was the greatest power she felt. It warmed her where the cracks were large inside her heart, the vessel that had been broken to pieces by grief and loss. "There will always be light," she thought, "even in my darkest times." I must allow this power that is true light in. With all of the destruction and loss this was a glimmer that grew into more than a glimmer. It became a guiding principle, a guiding light as she healed from the worst that had ever happened.

Hummingbird Words
Blanche Abrams

A typewriter clicks words of lost love
While hummingbird wings flitter
Into a fiery ember evening

Fingers fly across keys clicking toward evening. Inky indentations embellish papyrus with romance. Her mind is flowing with a searing novel. She can't type fast enough. Age is encroaching, rusting ideas as she searches for elusive words.

A dry scent causes her head to lift. Did she forget to turn off the burner? That sound. Like a crackling of trees, falling of branches. She sniffs the air, wipes her nose. On arthritic legs she hobbles to the window. Her spectacles light up with a chrysanthemum red hue.

"Oh, my love," she murmurs. "I wish you were here to see this sky. Remember how we sat on the porch swing at twilight?" She steadies herself at the sink. "A few hummingbirds would still be whirring their wings. 'They stopped by for an early nightcap,' you used to say. You would shoo away the feisty one so others had a chance at the feeder. You loved their comings and goings." A tear escapes from beneath her glasses. "Then when the day darkened we watched the red sun meet the horizon and slowly burn away. I'm certain certain you remember as much as I do."

She returns to her oak desk and antiquated typewriter, her words of love caressing the keys, though decreasing in speed. Flickering shadows of red flit about the house. She rests her silver head on her arm.

"I'll see you soon, my hummingbird man," she whispers. As she closes her eyes, her last breath leaves with a smile.

Flames lick across the keys of the writing machine. It is transfigured, one side lifting off the table as if in flight. The keys melt leaving only jagged edge fingers with thoughts never written. A partial sliver of paper is molded to the roller with her final love words. And when the fire subsides, the azure sky reappears and she is found alongside the typewriter, her hand enclosed over a crystalized hummingbird.

The Mixing Bowl
Blanche Abrams

Will Mosgrove

She sifts the ashes in search of life before the fire. Anything I find will be a comfort, she tells herself. Colors are all melded together in the ashen-hued lite and dark grey artifacts. Brown oak rafters once magnificent, now charred, are dark splinters of their former selves. Favorite statues have morphed into colorless disfigured shapes. Nothing is as it was. Something, please. There has to be something left. She can't accept every memory is burned. That the past she knew here in Grandma's house is gone.

Clouds shift, the sun's rays break through. A sparkle of color refracts, bounces back a brilliant, eye glaring blue. It can't be. It can't be, but it is. Grandma's mixing bowl. It was in the house for as long as she could remember. What memories it stirs within her. The scent of yeast mixed with warm water rising in the morning air.

The sound of the dough being whacked against the kitchen table. Grandma's apron and stout body dusted with white flour as she sang a Russian song, then blended thick oatmeal cookie mixture with a fat wooden spoon.

The bowl could also be found on the porch in the cool of evening, used for storage of pierogis or left over chicken soup with homemade noodles. Everything of Grandma's had dual function-especially the bowl.

Oh, it's not burned but it's broken. Some shards lay nearby in the ashes. She carefully picks them up. I can glue these pieces into place. Display the bowl on a shelf in my kitchen. Look at it and visit with Grandma whenever I want. Not everything ends. I made it through this fire as did the mixing bowl. We're both slightly broken, but we're here.

Breathing deeply, she coughs from lingering smoke and looks around as she clings to the bowl. Utter devastation stretches for acres. The house, trees, barn, silo, and fences are gone. I'm glad Grandma is not alive to witness this, she murmurs. She worked so hard. With nine children to care for she knew nothing of life save the constant creating and maintaining of it.

I can still see her standing in that tiny kitchen. Her face belied her years. Gardenia white skin was held taunt by high cheekbones. The only creases in her face were at the corners of her twinkling sea blue eyes. Her short hair ending just above her collar was shiny silver, looking like it could glow in the dark.

She always wore a long sleeve, milk colored undershirt which came out the armholes of her sleeveless, purple flowered dress. Coffee shaded, rolled up stockings showed beneath the hemline. They seemed to fall down farther the later the day became. You could practically tell time by them. Heavy black thick soled shoes supported her arthritic legs.

It's difficult to say if she had her figure due to layers of concealing clothing. The fact that her right breast had been removed years earlier went undetected. All she knew was when Grandma hugged her, she became lost in the warm lumpiness of her.

Grandma would be sad sometimes, as her children, on their own or away at college, didn't notice her aging. They were adrift in a sea of busy lives, families, and friends. She wasn't able to travel, to feel soft Hawaiian sand between her toes, or the coolness of pearls on her skin, or savor the texture of lobster.

She would sometimes say, "I wish my kids would buy me one of those newfangled washing machines and dryers," as she stood for hours with the old wringer machine and then hung all her clothes by hand.

Grandma died on a Saturday when her weary heart stopped beating. There was no school that day so she hadn't stopped by to say, "Hey, Grandma, whatcha fixin in your kitchen?" Aunt Jean had found her on the floor. Her wooden spoon still in her hand. The mixing bowl lay unbroken by her side. They had both served a lifetime of wear.

Beneath the smoky sky and amidst the ashes, her body shudders. Sobbing waves flow till there are no more tears to shed. She clutches the broken, but priceless bowl to her chest; a slight smile flickers, then she walks away without looking back.

When the Music Stopped
Cynthia Restivo

Will Mosgrove

Sitting on the blackened earth, she took a moment to cradle the clarinet's skeleton. She ran her fingers over the hole burned through the wall of the bell, the pads fused closed, and the jagged end where a mouthpiece had once been. She closed her eyes to remember when the clarinet sprang to life: when Gramps' moustached lips embraced the mouthpiece and made it swing; when Brother squeaked through clenched teeth; when Daughter's lips encircled the mouthpiece to play her first tentative tones, full of expectation and promise.

But the fire silenced the clarinet and the music stopped.

Will Mosgrove

Collectibles
Denella Kimura

Mary, Mary, quite contrary!
That's my name too.
I like playing with my doll house.
My house is special. It has a gray ceramic sink.
I made a plastic tub to go with it.
Santa's sleigh is on the rooftop
And Santa is inside putting presents
Under the Christmas tree.
Mom said I'm named after a queen: Queeeen
Mary!
She didn't like people much. Nor do I.
My friends are my dolls. My China baby
Named Mary, like me, fits in the cradle.
How does your garden grow?
With silver bells and cockle shells
Mine has a birdbath and a bird. He's a teal duck.
I made him a birdbath out of a cockleshell.
My Chinese Papa lives in the house too.
He eats a lot of rice in his bowl. I like rice.
And he wears a blue kimono too.
He has a long black pigtail down his back.
I like to braid it. But Daddy's hair is short.
And pretty maids all in a row.
Mommyyyy!? My doll house is burned
And my China dolls have lost their heads!

Sandbox
Denella Kimura

RRRRRR-RRRRR-EEEEE-BRKSHSHSH!
"Jamieeee! Time to come in!"
RRRR-RR-RRRR-PFTSSS!
"All right, Mommy! Just a minute."

"Jaime? Can you smell the smoke?"
"It's alright, Mommy." EEEEEEE!
"I've got a fire truck! And a bulldozer!"
RRRRRRR-EEEEEEE-WHOOSH!

"Jamie, there's a fire somewhere
Over by Butte Mountain! See it?"
"I can put it out with my fire truck, Mommy!"
WHOOSH! WHOOSH! WHOOSH! WHOOSH!

"Jamieee! I'm packing some clothes.
The fire's too close. Look! The neighbors
Are leaving! Hurry!"
RRRRRRRRRRRRRRRR-EEEEEK!
"I put the fire out, Mommy."

"Jamie, take my hand, honey. We've got to go NOW!"
"Okay, Mommy. Can I take my fire truck and tractor?"
"Sorry, honey. There's no more room in the car."

Will Mosgrove

Swag Box
Denella Kimura

I hide marble treasures in my swag box
    with my pint of ale. Harrrrr!
See the big "pearlie" with the dent in it?
That's the shooter I bammed all the others
    out of the dirt circle like a cannon:
        yellow, blue, green and red agates
           two-toned cats' eyes
                all mine, fair and square!
My treasure chest rusted
    flame marbled inside and out
      lock broken, useless.
What kept people out, the fire burst apart
    and drank up my stash of "ale"
      like a coca cola addict
    leaving behind my cracked glass "jug"
      bent, sucked in and twisted.
Melted marbles cling together like forlorn children
    sprinkled with ashes like snow
      their reformed eyes wiser because
    it's not a child's game
      anymore.

Will Mosgrove

Will Mosgrove

Temple of Pins
Monika Rose

Imagine the panic of pins
Their eyes wide, seeking escape
Trapped in a red pincushion

They brace for the rage and fiery heat
Alone, together like that
Huddled apart, stuck in every direction

A cherished thimble perches nearby
Illusive protection from the needle and
Errant ways of the seamstress

She fondles the cherished quilt with
No room for unfinished warmth in a
Crowded car, lets it fall back on the bed

Then gathers necessities, a toothbrush
Crumpled clothing, a dog dish, jewelry box,
A potato peeler her mother gave her

But what of the lowly pins?

That would come in time
When a gentle hand digs into ash
And makes her desire the thimble again

And there are the pins!
Survivors melted together,
As the community melded

Fused into a single rusty mass
Forgotten as instruments that
Hold, bind, connect

The forced collective
Of a pile of pins
Stuck together like this

But for fire, we won't know
What will stay
Past the going

The quilt gone, sewing basket
Burned, threads not even a whisper
The scissors—Where are they?

She breathes in the original scent
Of the garden, past scorched tang
And remembers white oaks and pine

Rock walls with nodding flowers
Miner's lettuce in clumps, mule's ears dancing
All this that once was, will again

More pins! More pins!

Out of the Fire, the Sea

Will Mosgrove

Monika Rose

So much transformation in once-cooking vessels, oven-safe,
After the fire passed, cooking them into sea creatures
A Corningware lid, sea slug of sorts, slips off the plate

Caught in a ripple of escape, in mid-wriggle
The slug, now a ray, and on its underside
A hint of mussel shell

A conch once a bowl, buffeted by flamewater,
Collapses unto itself, a shell dreaming wings
An orange hawk, shrouded in splash fire

A plate, twisted into abalone flesh, maybe
Once soft at the moment of intense heat
Now hardened into shell, with trying wings

The heat at 4,000 degrees past the limit
The vessels could not have fathomed the boil
The sheer melt ahead

They can rest secure in this new form,
For what could possibly harm them now?
Surely not fire, nor wind, nor movement of earth

No consumption, no swallowing, no biting here
They are untouchable, safe, waiting for a distant
Wave to move them somewhere else

I reach out and cradle the conch in loving awe
Of what it has endured, feel the heat of my hands
In a light warming, no danger of singeing or searing

The only terror left could be a shattering fall
A smattering of pieces reduced once more
But even this thought does not seem to faze the sea slug

It seems to say, "I have always been a piece made
To fit into another, and now your hand suits me."

The others whisper, a wave is coming, and we are
Heavy enough to roll to another place.
We have been there before, been here before

The sea slug transforms once again into
An ancient fish before my eyes
A dark, primitive blind bottom feeder

This will happen to us, it whispers
To you, and see, what is the worst
That could possibly ever be?

Will Mosgrove

Simple Cup
Monika Rose

So much depends upon
A vessel once, its handle
A delicate, curved arc with
Someone fingering the glaze
As tea sloshes into a saucer

I wonder about fingers that
Reach into cold ash and find partial form
Body tunneled and caved in,
Missing a center, then remember
An action of lifting, then setting down

This relic of embodiment,
Still, the memories in the cabinet silent
And stories at the table resound
Around breakfast on coffee mornings
Steaming cocoa afternoons

If you look closely at the melted glass
There on the handle, a ghost of fire appears
An O of surprise, caught in not a scream,
But a wry twist, a grimace
Its spirit snagged into revelation

Once I see the ghostly apparition
It will not tear away from imagination,
An echo of usefulness, haunting my very being
My hands surround the fragment, fingers tingle,
Ache to complete the broken circle

Monika Rose

Manzanita Writers Press has been serving the community
for over 30 years. A fledgling writers group blossomed into
a creative community center whose mission is to nurture and
sustain the literary and arts community of
Calaveras County and the foothill region.

Proceeds from this book will assist in funding
Manzanita's historic website, blog, and writing workshops
to help the community heal from the devastating Butte Fire of 2015.

MWP's goal is to help nurture new writers
and assist authors in reaching their publishing dream.

Home of Manzanita Writers Press

1211 South Main Street, Suite 110
Angels Camp, California 95222
(209)728-6171

Contributor Notes

Blanche Abrams, a writer living in Columbia, CA, is a member of the Sonora Writers Group. Her short stories, essays, and poetry have been published in several literary anthologies, including MWP's publication, *Wine, Cheese, and Chocolate.* She is working on a collection of aviation fiction.

Sydney Avey, author of *The Sheep Walker's Daughter* and *The Lyre and the Lambs,* lives in Groveland, in the Yosemite area of the Sierra Nevada and in Arizona's Sonoran Desert.

Kathleen Ball of the Mother Lode holds a Ph.D. in Philosophy of Metaphysical Sciences and has traveled extensively to visit archeological digs. In addition to hosting a television program, she has enjoyed a career in painting and sculpture. She has taught at Columbia College and designed art programs for the central Sierra Foothills area.

Donna Becker is a family law attorney and mediator, grandmother, Zen practitioner, occasional botanical artist and poet residing in Santa Cruz and recently Murphys. She has published in *Porter Gulch Review, Phren-Ze Online Literary Magazine* and read at the Santa Cruz Celebration of the Muse.

Michelle Bellinger, living in San Andreas, CA, has been photographing Family Milestones from birth through the end of life for the past 15 years and for the past 24 years has specialized in photo restoration of old photographs that are damaged and faded with time. She worked for the San Andreas Fire Department for 10 years as their photographer. Genealogy is a passion she has worked on for the past 32 years and photography is a natural step in documenting a family's life. Thus, the two passions have become one.

Helen Bonner was a resident of Mountain Ranch many years before the fire and resided in Jackson. She holds a Ph.D. in literature and has written and published several books and many poems over the years. A University professor for many years, she is now retired and lives in Stockton

Maria Camillo, a Murphys resident, has been a full-time music business professional since 1989, working for music festivals, as a booking agent, and concert promoter/talent buyer. She has photographed music festivals and concerts across the country, does photography and graphic design for CD packages, and enjoys travel photography.

Wayne Carlson has lived in Railroad Flat for seven years, and photography has always been a passion of his since he was a 12-year-old growing up in Newark, CA. A retired truck driver from the Bay area, he lives with his wife Kim in Railroad Flat. All his photos are spontaneous moments, as he carries his camera with him everywhere.

Ty Childress, a Mountain Ranch resident and retired teacher, travels all over the country to capture professional photography of natural landscapes and wildlife, as well as rural scenes. He and his wife operate an organic farm, and his property was heavily damaged in the Butte Fire, but the disaster prompted him to record the poignant beauty in destruction. His photography is shown at Manzanita Arts Emporium in Angels Camp.

Katie Clark is Creative Director at "Lapcats: Matching Pets with People" whose mission is to provide support and resources to the Bradshaw Animal Shelter by reaching a broader community rescuing, rehabilitating, fostering, showcasing, and adopting shelter cats at off-site venues.

Connie Collins, a retired lady, a mother and a grandmother, lives south of Jackson, CA on 40 acres. Her family has a small farm at the end of a dirt road. She lives with her husband, two Corgis, three goats, a cat and a flock of chickens. She loves where she has landed and says that life is good.

Anne Cook is a lifelong artist and junk collector whose professional work includes illustration, graphic design, jewelry making and teaching. People can find her at Acme Art Studio in Mokelumne Hill, a creative arts center. She is co-artist of the Pieces Project

Constance Corcoran is a retired librarian. She spent her childhood in Calaveras County. Self-published works, *The Red and the Blonde* and *Gumption: A Grandmother's Story*, include stories of Calaveras County in the 1950s. Her poems appear in previous issues of *Manzanita*. She lives with her husband in Tuolumne, CA.

Wayne Carlson

Cate Culver comes from the fourth generation of a California family. Her home in the Gold Rush Country provides her with inspiration and rich subject matter. Cate's semi-abstract paintings, incorporating bright colors and natural design elements, flow with the drama of the Sierra Nevada land forms.

Brent Duffin, from the Davis area, is a former, now retired, Advisor with the Intensive English Program at U.C. Davis, Extension. The *Out of the Fire* project reminds him that the words that we give to things do matter and do make a difference—at least on a personal level. Most of the images in the collage depicted in the book were taken in a single shooting.

Gordon Long

Pam Dunn lives and writes in Paso Robles, CA, and is working on two novels. She published her prize-winning short story "Sunflowers" in *Suisun Valley Review* #32. "Who Reads Anymore" was published in *Wine, Cheese, and Chocolate,* Winter, 2014. She has degrees in Creative Writing and Library Science.

Kat Everitt, poet, community activist, and songwriter, hosts "Everywoman's Hour" on local radio station KQBM and makes her home in Pioneer. Her columns frequently appear in local newspapers and periodicals.

Rebecca Fischer was raised in Calaveras County. She studied English and Multimedia at Columbia College and helps out on her family's ranch. She is also currently researching her great-grandparents' love story, with the intent of writing a biography about them.

George Haskell has always loved landscape painting, especially capturing in oil the grandeur of the Yosemite Valley. George makes his home just outside Murphys on the top of Treasure Mountain.

Shannon Jewel lives in Calaveras County where she works as the Copperopolis Library Branch Assistant.

Denella Kimura has two poetry books, *Poetry Reading at the Panama Hotel* and *Waiting for Wings: A Child's Journey.* She has published chapbooks, articles, devotionals, book reviews and drama. She moderates "Open Reading at Sonora Joe's," and produces two radio programs, "Favorite Things" and "Coffee House Writers" for KAAD-LP, Sonora.

Kent Lambert and his wife Darcy moved to Mokelumne Hill in 1991 to raise their family. Their house and property burned on Day Two of the Butte Fire, and they will be moving back home in summer 2017. When he is not working to restore and rebuild their 21 acres, Kent works for East Bay Municipal Utility District to manage the watershed and recreation programs at Pardee and Camanche Reservoirs. His photography captured the Butte Fire aftermath.

Conrad Levasseur has made his home in Calaveras County since 1981 and works in community relations and development at Ironstone Vineyards in Murphys.

Gordon Long, professional photographer, grew up on the ridge near West Point in the Mokelumne River Canyon. His family doesn't still live at the childhood residence, but his roots in the community of Mokelumne Hill run deep. It was extremely rewarding for him to go back to the fire scar and document, through photography, the rebirth of the environment over an 18-month span after the fire ended.

Gayle Lorraine, intuitive abstract artist, makes her home in Calaveras County and has placed her works in local galleries.

M.J. Mallery, of Stockton, taught English in Istanbul and did secretarial work for KABL radio in San Francisco. While volunteering for her father in Stockton, she developed a passion for exploring nature in the Sierra Nevada. M.J. Mallery is a member of Writers Unlimited.

Robin Modlin, is a mosaic and healing artist and lives in Livermore and Murphys, CA. She has always loved the message that mosaic brings of putting together the broken to make a new more beautiful whole. She is also a SoulCollage® facilitator. Robin creates community art as well as individual works. She is co-artist of the Pieces Project.

Will Mosgrove joined the Academy of Art University in 2006 as Director of Graduate Photography, capping 30 years as a professional photographer. He volunteered with American Photographic Artists (APA) where he served as National President for three terms. In 2008, Mosgrove was awarded APA's 25th anniversary leadership award and in 2009 he received the prestigious International Photographic Council's Leadership Award, which was presented at the United Nations.

Suzanne Murphy, retired English instructor and Public Relations Director of Manzanita Writers Press, lives in Valley Springs. She is a member of Writers Unlimited.

Debora Olguin, photographer, musician, and professional vocalist, lives in Angels Camp and chronicled the Butte Fire in a sequence of photos taken during its first ten days of devastation.

Nitya Prema, from Avery, CA, has a psychotherapy practice in Angels Camp. After returning from evacuation of her home during the Butte Fire, she treated several fire trauma cases. She is finalizing her memoir for publication titled, *Through the Tibetan Mirror: A Kaleidoscope of Consciousness.*

Cynthia Restivo, a professional storyteller, enjoys listening to stories as much as telling them. She teaches storytelling in Stockton and is a freelance artist throughout Northern California. She co-produced two award-winning CDs, *Storyquilters* and *Blackberry Love,* and published *Hanging On.* Cynthia is currently working on another book, *Fire Stories.*

Monika Rose, of Mountain Ranch, founded Manzanita Writers Press and is published in several anthologies and literary magazines. Her book of poems, *River by the Glass,* by GlenHill Publications, will soon be accompanied by a novel and a collection of short fiction. She is an Adjunct Associate Professor of English at Delta College.

Mark Russell lives in the Sierra Foothills and has enjoyed backpacking with his family and owning a Jetta.

Selma Sattin, watercolorist, lives in Copperopolis and shows her original work, prints, and cards in the Manzanita Arts Emporium. She teaches watercolor painting classes to young artists at the gallery.

Ann Seely has always written, journaling since she was a little girl, waiting to have something to write about. She figures it's about time to start. She lives with her husband, two teenagers, two dogs and an aging cat-muse, in San Andreas. She is writing a San Francisco-based historical novel.

Don Seeman, residing in Calaveras County, took photos of the Butte Fire in the dramatic month of September 2015. His photography will appear in an upcoming book about the fire.

Maggie Sloan, a Mother Lode artist, illustrator, and writer living in Murphys, is assistant to the executive director at Calaveras County Arts Council, and is in charge of marketing and social media. She is a member of Writers Unlimited in Angels Camp. She believes that life should be an art project.

John Slot, a freelance photographer living in Rancho Calaveras, experienced nine days that changed his life forever during the Butte Fire. His photos were aired on local, state and national news. He opened John Slot Photography in 2014, after studying natural photography at Columbia College. He quickly rose to become one of the top selling photographers in the Western US.

Gail Stark has always considered herself to be an integral part of her natural surroundings, sharing the land upon which she lives with the myriad slithering, crawling, walking, and flying creatures of her neighborhood. She understands that the Butte Fire left its devastating mark on so many lives in the Mother Lode, including her own.

Pru Starr was born in Tokyo, Japan. She earned her Master's degree in Reading and Language Arts, and taught on Prince of Wales Island in South East Alaska and in Northern California. Pru and her husband have a ranch in Calaveras County, and she writes about home, heart, and work

Linda Toren, retired teacher from Calaveras Unified School District, has lived for forty years in West Point on a small farm with her family. She volunteers at West Point and Rail Road Flat Schools on year-long poetry projects. She belongs to Pine Grove Writers Group and Licensed Fools writing group in Modesto.

Charleen Tyson lives in the beautiful summer-blonde foothills of the Sierra Nevada range in Northern California where the deer, foxes and wild turkeys roam free. They get enough snow to be reminded how beautiful it is, but not so much that she doesn't look forward to it each year.

Caitlin Wilbur lives in the fire-ravaged Mountain Ranch area and lost her beloved home. She has a GoFundMe site to help her and Jack rebuild.

Joy Willow, a Sonora resident who has an active studio in her home, describes her work in mixed-media as abstract renderings of interior landscapes that emerge from meditations on the natural world. Her paintings provide a balance with the verbal arts of song and poetry.

Sarah Wilson lives in Murphys, CA, where she experienced the fears of evacuation first-hand, and she was able to give firefighters directions as to where they needed to go, most likely instilling in her young three-year-old the vital importance of firefighters to the survival of our community.

Jerry Zellers has lived most of his life in the Gold Country area. He is a 30-year-old musician, writer, and firefighter currently making his home in Mokelumne Hill.

Gordon Long

Wayne Carlson

"For a while, we hold a piece of Eden or Shangri-La,
or whatever pure, safe place we want to call it,
in our own world."
　　　Monika Rose